Good-by My Son

Good-by My Son

"A father tells of the agony and the spiritual stren, revealed as death stalked his 21-year-old son."

Erwin Paul Rudolph

ZONDERVAN PUBLISHING HOUSE

OF THE ZONDERVAN CORPORATION | GRAND RAPIDS, MICHIGAN 49506

Good-by, My Son

© Copyright 1971 by Zondervan Publishing House
Grand Rapids, Michigan

Fifth printing   September 1975

Library of Congress Catalog Card Number 72-153463

Printed in the United States of America

To
JAMES, Zeke's only brother,
whose sense of irreplaceable loss
will likely be the most prolonged

Contents

Preface

This is a story about death. But it is even more a story about life. What began with promise and hope ended early and seemingly without fulfillment. A life that was just beginning to unfold and develop was suddenly stilled by powers beyond its control. And yet something in man refuses to accept that end as final. Golden threads of immortality and glory interlace our innermost thoughts as we look beyond the grave to the One "who hath abolished death, and hath brought life and immortality to light through the gospel." [1]

We do not pretend to understand why God's time-table differed so markedly from our own. But it was ours which was out of adjustment, not His. "As the heavens are higher than the earth, so are my ways higher than your ways, and my thoughts than your thoughts." [2] At long last we shall know, even as we are known. But "now we see through a glass, darkly." [3]

This book is meant to offer understanding and comfort to others who have lost a loved one. It is also intended to speak to youth about the wise assessment of values, thoughtful alignment of life's priorities, and early contemplation of holy things. We pray earnestly that the life which appeared here so briefly will not be like a bubble that appears for a time on the surface of the wave and then vanishes forever, but rather will remind other young people like our son that mere length of life avails little in the light of eternity — that, instead, the intensity and quality of the days spent on earth are what matter most of all. Surely, the God of beauty and youth sees and loves the young person who seeks Him early — before the weight of years has bowed down the soul with evil habits and neglect.

Perhaps our son's testimony in these pages will compensate in part for the days he was denied on earth. If many who contemplate his words and example are turned toward God, he will have accomplished in death a worthy and far-reaching goal.

As we knew Erwin Paul II, he would rebuke us for grieving too long, even though he knows we love him more than our own lives. Neither would he choose to return to the same physical limitations, the same devastating weakness which was his final lot in life. God was kind to release him from physical infirmity. Even more, Erwin would prod us to think about the future, to order our lives here in accord with the Divine Purpose, and to help others find their spiritual bearings. His spirit beckons us to follow onward and upward in God's ways.

The personal pronoun "I" will abound in these pages because I, Erwin's father, am telling the story. The frequent use of "we" will be more than an editorial reference, for it will include his mother, June, who shares equally with me not only the pain and loss, but also the Christian consolation and hope. She has been my chief consultant, and without her help and encouragement I could not have completed this task.

E. P. R.

*Life
Aglow*

1.

Life Aglow

WHEN I FIRST LEARNED the truth that a vicious marauder was to invade our home and threaten the life of one of its members, I was hardly prepared to accept it.

I had witnessed a great deal of suffering and death in my lifetime and was no stranger to adversity; nevertheless I was guilty of taking good health merely for granted. All four members of our family had been relatively free from long-term illness. I am sure we had given some serious thoughts to these matters, but reading about sickness or death in the newspaper or even seeing it happen to others from a distance is far different from encountering it personally. The common tendency is to view mortality as human, but remote. As Thomas Young tells us in *Night Thoughts*, "All men think all men mortal but themselves."

However, in a swift stroke one can be made vividly aware of how frail and unsure life is — that "there is but a step between me and death" (I Sam. 20:3).

Our two sons, James and Erwin Paul II (Zeke), at twenty-seven and twenty, respectively, were lithe and strong, the former with almost 175 pounds hung on a six-foot, one-inch frame, and the latter, five-feet, ten inches, and about ten pounds lighter. Both admitted to an exceptional weakness for their mother's Sunday roast-beef dinners. Zeke's preference for hamburgers was matched only by his love for ice cream. I complained once to our pediatrician that I thought Zeke's diet lacked proper balance for a growing boy — that he ate too many hamburgers and hot dogs and not enough vegetables and fruit. He replied that the body was its own best gauge of its needs. From that time forward I let nature have its own way.

Both of our sons were larger and stronger than their father. That, however, did not stop me from challenging them occasionally to a wrestling match. I had been used to doing this during their growing years when my strength was still superior, but when the balance of power shifted dramatically, my attacks became more of a nuisance than a threat. By unspoken, gentlemen's agreement, whatever showing I made after that time was due to their deference for my fatherly status.

Then came the bomb.

Our physician had called earlier in the day to request an immediate conference. The note of urgency in his voice had led me to suspect he had found out something more definite from the recent hospital tests taken on Zeke. Up to this point the symptoms had baffled general practitioners and specialists alike. The long, arduous path over months of intermittent hospitalizations and tests more than hinted at an ominous diagnosis, but in the face of uncertainty one always hopes for the best.

Though my own health was perfect, it had never occurred to me that I might survive one of my children. As with our older son, so with Zeke: he was so very much alive. Physically strong and mentally alert, he personified vitality, youth, promise, hope. Not unlike thousands of other young men of his age, he was vibrant, eager, and enthusiastic. His special zest for life and his marked ability to extract the nectar from every moment enhanced the love of life for those around him.

I remember my response after the doctor disclosed to me that our son had an incurable disease. It was as though I were struck from several sides simultaneously. My senses reeled and a general numbness stole over my body. I scarcely heard the doctor's comments which followed. Vaguely, I recall his pointing to a chart of the nervous system and explaining something of the nature of the disease, of the unpredictability of its course throughout the body after its initial attacks, and of how many people who have it continue to lead near-normal lives for many years. He offered me some pamphlets to read, which were designed to allay my fears and help me to assume a positive outlook.

Although I tried to listen, my mind simply would not follow a steady course. How does one parry a gigantic blow and prepare to rebuild in a moment upon the ashes still aglow from the fires of a former dream?

After the interview I walked dazedly to the car and began the fifteen-mile drive from the doctor's office in Oak Park to Wheaton. Driving home that day was much more habit and reflex than conscious act. Still numb from the blow I had just sustained, my mind began to wander surrealistically through a variety of subjects — the implications of the doctor's words, conjecture about the future, the confusion of recent events. Then it began to turn back through the short chapters of Zeke's early years to the very beginning. . . .

Life began for Erwin Paul II (Zeke) on October 8, 1947, in Toledo, Ohio. His arrival produced considerable elation in our home, for it had been seven years since the birth of our first son, and we were ready for number two. I was pastor of a church in Toledo at the time, so Zeke had an early introduction to parsonage life.

A few months later we accepted a call from my alma mater in Greenville, Illinois, to fill a vacancy in the English Department caused by a teacher on sabbatical leave. Zeke had no recollection of that experience, as we remained there only one year. From Greenville we went to the Chicago suburb of Melrose Park to assume another pastorate. From there, the family's paths turned once more toward Christian education — this time to Wheaton College in Illinois, where we were to stay more or less permanently and where Zeke was to complete most of his formative years.

This sandy-haired, fair-complexioned gift from God may have had no claim to exceptional talents or rare promise, but he found a ready entrance into our hearts.

As he was growing up, Zeke was not an easy boy to handle. He had a mind of his own which made for stubbornness and intractability. Characteristically, he followed a leisurely pace and procrastinated in his studies to the point of exasperation. I scolded him repeatedly for this and even resorted to corporal punishment when he was smaller, but neither proved effective. That he recognized his fault is shown in an entry in his journal:

> *November 12, 1965:* "Why do I do these things? Three hours of cramming for a history test does not prepare one for a big exam! Why can't I learn to spread out my study time and really be ready. . . . I am going to turn over a new leaf and budget my time more efficiently."

Alas, firm resolution failed.

Although very clean in his person and meticulous about his appearance, Zeke was extremely careless about hanging up his clothes and did little to prevent the disorderly array in his room. We often teased him about it, but he didn't seem to attach importance to this kind of detail.

Naturally, as we planned for his future, we thought in terms of a normally long life. Since Zeke was not to have many years here, his acts now take on new significance. Probably the intense manner of life he lived for those twenty-one years was because he unconsciously heard "time's winged chariot drawing near."

In a way, father, mother, and sons grew up together. June and I had no time-tested formula about how to rear children. We had taken no courses in "marriage" nor had we read any books on family care. We may have done fairly well in keeping up pious exercises in our home, but again, whatever success we may claim in raising our boys was hardly traceable to our laudable example or superior indoctrination.

Our family simply liked to do things together. When one of the boys took part in a school play or participated in the band or gave a recitation in church, the other members were foremost as spectators and critics. Since Zeke's most singular achievements were to be in athletics, we had many opportunities to share in the competitions and to engage in lively discussions afterward. As interested parents, we learned much about all kinds of sports. Most of all, the athletic events gave us a common meeting ground and the opportunity to become a closely-knit family unit.

The nickname "Zeke" came about in an unusual way. It was in the spring of 1954 that we were moving our household goods from Melrose Park to Wheaton via "U-Drive It" truck. Each of us was in a holiday mood and singing and joking as we carried goods into the house. Some of the neighborhood children were spectators of the grand operation. I happened to be singing parts of "Ezekiel saw the wheel away in the middle of the air." Once I called out, "Hey, Ezekiel." One of the neighbor boys caught it. I actually spoke the name only once or twice, but Ezekiel was quickly shortened to "Zeke" and the nickname was fashioned suddenly and unexpectedly. Nicknames may be attached for various and illogical reasons, but Zeke didn't mind his at all. In fact, he preferred it to both "Erwin" and "Paul" and often signed his nickname on papers throughout high school and college. Some of his good friends never knew but what "Zeke" was his real name.

Zeke always made friends easily. In fact, the ease and rapidity with which he formed social ties became one of his distinguishing characteristics. Both our boys always felt free to bring their friends to our home, either singly or in groups, to get a snack, have a game of ping-pong, play the stereo or shoot baskets on the backyard court. Zeke also had his close friends, like Don and Chuck, who were to be found in his company more than the others. Many have written notes to me or have come by our home or office to comment on what Zeke's friendship has meant to them. One boy said, "He was always a lot of fun; yet I knew there was a very deep, serious side to him." A girl about his own age said, "I knew him quite well and liked the things he stood for. He could laugh, but his fun was of the wholesome sort."

One of Zeke's close friends, Dale Frank, recalls several associations:

> Zeke and I were introduced in junior high school, but it wasn't until high school that we became good friends. . . . As high schoolers, we were very active in sports, dates, choir and just hacking around . . . .
> I always respected Zeke as an athlete. He had a subtle way of appearing very relaxed and passive and then sur-

prising the opposition with a sudden spurt of energy. . . .
He was instrumental in leading our church basketball squad
to its championship in 1965. . . .

Zeke was in choir, although not a regular participant. . . .
I remember his leaning toward me and pointing out the
attractive qualities of the girls in the front row. I ended
up marrying one of them. . . .

We had lots of fun on double dates. Sometimes we took
the girls to a haunted house on the southwest side of
Wheaton and ended up scaring ourselves. . . . Again, the
fellows would pile into my V.W. and Rich Scott's Triumph
and Zeke's Tempest and go for a race and end up at one
of our favorite eating spots on Roosevelt Road. There we
would goof off. . . . Zeke had a quiet sense of humor; it
wasn't so much what he said as the way he said it that
was so funny. He would explode with a sudden laugh and
the rest of us would roll with laughter. . . . He was happy-
go-lucky and a lot of fun to be with.

How could one reflect upon Zeke's early life without re-
calling some of his associations with Little League and Pony
League baseball?

Little League baseball was highly competitive in the Whea-
ton-Glen Ellyn area. This was the era of fiery managers, irate,
vocal parents, and screaming players. Umpiring was an un-
envied, if not hazardous, occupation. Nevertheless, the boys
learned much about the game and how to compete under
pressure. Little League baseball has been assailed as too
emotional and pressure-ridden for eleven to fourteen-year-
old boys. Too often, the critics say, parents interfere with
the conduct of the game and impose their own demands
upon coach and player to the detriment of the child. June
and I were much involved with the sport, but we always
felt that if parents and coaches kept the boys' interests and
welfare uppermost, the competition offered an excellent preparation for life.

Zeke had been asked by the managers to play in some of

the "major" league's games even when he was a "minor" leaguer, for he was considered more than an average threat with a bat in his hand. One of the most vivid recollections I have of any single batting performance was at an All-Star game in Glen Ellyn when as an eleven-year-old he hit the first ball pitched over the left-field fence for a home run. After circling the bases he dashed into the dugout and shouted excitedly to his surprised teammates, "You guys can hit that pitcher; he doesn't have a thing." A little eleven-year-old lead-off man playing his first game in the majors was telling the veterans how to play ball!

The following selections from his scrapbook tell some of the Little League story:

Rudolph Tops Cats, Cubs Tie for Lead

A brilliant no-hit pitching effort by Rudolph enabled the Cubs to beat the Wildcats 4 to 0 and throw the second half race for the Red division title in the Wheaton Little league into a three-way deadlock for first place.

Rudolph blanked the previously unbeaten Wildcats without a hit or run, while his Cub teammates were scoring four runs on three hits. One of the hits were Harding's inside-the-park home run.

Bruins Belt Wildcats, Rudolph Slams Homer

Erwin Rudolph slammed a home run and hurled a three hitter to lead the Cubs to an 11 to 3 victory over the Wildcats in Wheaton Little League action this week.

It was the first win of the season for the once powerful Cubs. They have dropped two. The winners tallied once in the firth inning, three times in the second, twice in the fifth and left no doubt about the outcome with a five run fifth inning. All the Wildcats' runs were scored in the last of the fifth.

Roger Schmidt's triple was the big blow for the losers.

In another game, the Tigers edged the Lions, 2 to 0. Bruce Ehlers hurled the shut-out.

Cubs 10, Colts 3 – Panthers Over Tigers

The division leading Cubs crushed the Colts Friday by a 10-3 score. Pitcher Rudolph of the Cubs led his team, hitting safely in all of his three times at bat, (one was a double) scoring two runs, and holding the Colts to five hits.

In the Panthers-Tigers game Friday, the opposing pitchers gave up only two runs each, but the Panthers made the most of what they had, defeating the Tigers 6-0.

Cubs (11)	AB	R	H	Colts (3)	AB	R	H
Kammes	3	1	1	Aldrich ..	3	1	1
Tichava	4	0	0	West	0	0	0
J. Natale	4	2	2	Stansfield	2	0	0
Rudolph	3	2	3	Borhely	0	0	0
Peters	3	1	0				
Johnson							

Badgers Win Crown, End Cub 'Dynasty'

A thrilling extra inning contest decided who the champions of the Wheaton Little League would be After a 2-2 tie with the Cubs the Badgers came across with the winning run when Jack Todd's infield bounder drove in John Neuenfeldt.

The game itself was the climax to the Wheaton Little League season, the Blue Division Champs, the Badgers, met the Red Division Cubs.

Starting pitchers of the two teams were "Mimi" Kee for the Badgers, and "Zeke" Rudolph for the Cubs, two of the best hurle n the league. After six innings, new pitchers were brought in and consequently Roger Williamson picked up the win while Larry Kammes was given the loss.

In the first inning, the Cubs threatened after Natale walked and then Rudolph singled. Kee, however, seemed to be in control as he got the final two outs in the inning with little trouble.

In the bottom of the first, the Badgers drew first blood. Kee, the leadoff batter, singled. He progressed to second on Glasser's singles, and then went to third when Neuenfeldt drew a walk. A fly ball to right gave Kee enough time to tag up and score the first run.

Although troubled with a stiff arm, Rudolph pitched consistent ball, as did Kee. The Cubs were retired in order in the second and third innings. The Badgers, however, loaded up the bases in the third inning, but were unable to score.

Rudolph's sharp double into left field failed to start a Cub rally in the fourth, and "Zeke" was left stranded on base.

"Mimi" Kee scored the second Badgers run of the night after a couple of Cub errors in the bottom of the fourth.

It looked as if the Cubs would wrap up the ball game in the fifth inning. With the bases loaded, Bill Scott scored after he and the Badger third baseman became entangled between third and home. Interference was called, bringing in Scott with the first Cub run.

This left the bases still full, and brought up the Cub powerhouse, "Zeke" Rudolph. With a resounding crack of the bat, "Zeke" let loose with a blow that looked like sure extra bases. Kee, however, reached far to his right and the ball hit his glove, the impact knocking the Badger pitcher tot he ground, but he held fast to the ball.

Kee regained his footing in time to fire the ball to third, catching the Cubs runner before he had a chance to get back.

This double play got the Badgers out of hot water.

After being walked, Rich Scott of the Cubs got to second on Harding's single. Scott tied-up the game at 2-2 when he scored on an overthrow.

Zeke's love for baseball continued into high school and college where he developed additional poise and self-confidence. The fact that he was one of two college freshmen who earned a varsity letter in baseball attests to his improved ability.

Daily Journal Sports

SCOTT HANSON   Sports Editor

Three "W" Local Men

Three Wheaton men were among the 100 sports letter winners at Wheaton College this spring.

They are senior Jay Hakes, 225 Kellogg, major letter in tennis; freshman Erwin P. Rudolph, 1005 Santa Rosa, major letter in baseball and minor letter in basketball; and junior Robert L. Unser, 1319 North President, minor letter in golf. Hakes served as captain of the varsity tennis team.

Eighty-one major letter and twenty-nine minor letters were presented to members of the baseball, basketball, golf, gymnastics, tennis, track, and wrestling teams at the college's athletic convocation. Seven athletes were double letter winners.

Additional insights into Zeke's early years are given in the recollections of Zeke's close friend and next-door neighbor, Berry Fiess:

Although I was about ten when Zeke and his family moved in next door, I cannot remember the moment we first met. Our neighborhood clique was slow in recognizing a newcomer, I'm afraid. But my earliest memories of him center around games of "spud," hide and seek, football, basketball, swimming, and "500". . . .

Each spring would bring talk of baseball, spring training, and baseball bubblegum cards. We would continually buy and trade cards, hoping to get a complete set of our favorite major league players. I remember seeing a complete set only once or twice, and one of them was Zeke's. He loved baseball.

On a typical summer evening we would round up the neighborhood fellows and play "500" on Old Lawson Field, yelling at the top of our voices, as competition became fierce. When hot weather came and most of the neighborhood kids lay around taking it easy, Zeke might be seen out pitching or hitting with Jim and his dad.

After most of us had played our summer hearts out and turned our thoughts to school, Zeke headed toward the basketball court. . . . Then he would come rounding up needed players for a "two on two" game. All of us labeled him a sports man.

One of the earliest football games we played with Zeke in our side yard was an eventful one. We did not know him very well then — nor his German Shepherd dog. My older brother was playing with us and when my brother went to tackle Zeke, his dog took a chunk out of my brother's leg. The game was ended when my brother began to howl and ran for first aid. We never played there again when Zeke's dog was loose. . . .

One summer afternoon as we were coming home from the swimming pool on our bikes, clad only in our swimming trunks, we came to a street that was being repaired with fresh tar. Instead of taking a detour, Zeke decided to take the short way home. When we finally met up with him, he was completely covered with tar. He headed for home and we heard later that he tried to wash the tar off in the shower. However, his mother had to subject him to more severe scrubbing in the basement laundry tubs.

It wasn't until I was fully aware of Zeke's condition that I first started to think deeply concerning him and his actions. All that had transpired between us somehow began to take on new meaning. I thought back upon the times we had enjoyed together in our neighborhood — even to the feuds we had had. Suddenly all of those kid-squabbles seemed so small. I see now a genuine Christian who had a well-defined job to perform for his Savior. His testimony has taken on new meaning.

Zeke loved other sports, too — basketball, golf, tennis and skiing. Always fiercely competitive, he admired and emulated those whose abilities were greater than his. His basketball talents were just beginning to unfold when his disability set in. His accurate shooting ability, which was perhaps his crowning asset, was made possible by long hours of practice on our lighted backyard basketball court. Boys of the neighborhood frequently played there until almost midnight.

The other freshman previously referred to who, along with Zeke, earned a varsity letter in baseball in 1966 was John Pierucki. John went on to become a star in basketball, also. Later he wrote the following as he recalled some of his associations with Zeke:

> Zeke and I first met in Centennial Gym my second day on Wheaton's campus. He impressed me greatly that day with his extreme quickness and uncanny accuracy in shooting. I can honestly say he had the best shot I had seen. The one thing he lacked most at that time in athletics was determination. He could have done much better had he had a better attitude.
>
> We became very close friends that first semester in 1965. Almost every night we would meet at the Student Center for ice cream. Neither of us took studying too seriously,

yet! By second semester we decided we would room together in the new Fischer Hall. It was at that time that I seemed to notice a change in Zeke. . . .

He began sleeping more than what seemed normal and went long periods without studying. I really felt sorry for him because I just couldn't get him motivated.

Zeke was very attentive — contrary to his relaxed manner. Outwardly, he was much concerned about his appearance. He dated quite a bit, but not seriously. He had very few enemies, if any.

He was a great guy. We had a lot of good talks, and I saw the compassionate, sensitive side of Zeke. Many people, including myself, thought him to be somewhat of a joker because he *appeared* to be unconcerned about so many things. But he was concerned and he did want very much to be accepted for what he was. He didn't like phonies and he could pick them out of any crowd. I guess it was because he was so "real" to me that his friendship meant a lot. I hated to think of him suffering physically, because I knew he would be suffering more deeply mentally.

It may be that Zeke thought too much about sports. Perhaps I did, too, and encouraged him excessively in this direction. I tended to justify myself and him on the grounds that vigorous physical activity was a natural deterrent to the dangers inherent in idleness. I also appreciated some of the fine associations which he formed and the lessons he learned in the sports world.

A sports camp in Connecticut which he attended as counselor in the summer of 1965 proved unusually beneficial to him. One of his former coaches invited him to go, and when we encouraged him to accept rather than stay home and work, he was surprised. The following excerpt is from a theme he wrote for Freshman Writing later that fall:

This past summer I began to notice and take an interest in the beauty of our land for the first time. This was made possible by the opportunity I had to counsel at a Christian basketball camp in Connecticut. Situated in the wilds of the mountains, the camp was ideally located for me to see outside my little world. . . .

The loveliness of the trees, sky, and streams moved me as they had never done before. Alone in the forest, I could almost feel God's presence . . . . Nature seemed to boast of God's creation.

I soon found a specific spot where I loved to go when I felt low or wanted to think. It was on a rock on top of a hill overlooking the valley and lake. Here all my frustrations and problems seemed to fade into obscurity. The beauty of nature . . . opened my eyes to more important horizons than the hustle of city life. . . . I began to realize the importance of slowing down and taking an interest in the little things around us. . . .

The following entry from his journal dated Monday, November 15, 1965, relates his response to a college athletic meeting:

My heart was really blessed and uplifted this afternoon during our first basketball squad meeting. Though at this initial meeting I didn't testify, I heard many of the others speak of what Jesus Christ meant to them personally. Their feelings and dedication to Him encouraged me to experience a closer walk with God. Whatever may become of the season, we are a team playing for Jesus Christ and His glory and not for ourselves. We're determined to work hard and play our best for Him.

There was no reason to believe that life for Zeke would be cut short. He was glowing with life. His body was strong and well-proportioned, his coordination and reflexes flawless.

He had no idea that his transfer from the basketball court and baseball diamond to "fresh woods" and "pastures new" would be so soon.

But the invader was stalking ever closer.

Shadows

2.

Shadows

Zeke's descent from the peak of health was gradual at first — sometimes almost imperceptible. Because the symptomatic changes occurred so slowly, he was inclined to minimize or misinterpret them. Even when it became clear that something was seriously wrong, the signs were still not distinctive enough to characterize a specific disease. The rarity of the malady that plagued him also helped to complicate the diagnosis.

Zeke's freshman year in college was normal in most respects. He managed to keep up in his studies (to this point in his life he had never been one who went all out for academic achievement) and to take part in the usual functions of campus life. He looked forward eagerly to try-outs for the baseball team and was invited to accompany the squad on its southern spring tour. Although he later disclosed that on this trip he first noticed his inability to throw a baseball as accurately as usual, he nevertheless could throw as hard as ever. Neither he nor his teammates paid much attention

to his lack of control, for he was characteristically wild —
even when he was a "little leaguer."

Zeke developed well enough for the coach to give him
several starting pitching assignments on the spring tour. Although he said nothing about it at the time, he told us later
that during periods of excitement even on the southern baseball trip he would see two baseballs coming toward him
instead of one. Usually the aberration was temporary, he
explained, so he ignored it.

We were not unduly alarmed when Zeke spoke to us of
the first signs of double vision, although he was not the sort
who complained about personal difficulties, unless they were
prominent and persistent. We also reasoned that whatever
he was experiencing was probably temporary and would
abate in time. Too, since he wore contact lenses, we reasoned
that something could be wrong with his lens' adjustment.

Following the regular academic year, in the summer of
1966, Zeke had the opportunity to attend the Wheaton College Science Station in the Black Hills. Many college students choose this way to fulfill part of their general education
requirements in science. The wilderness setting affords opportunities not only for studying geology, but also for hiking,
swimming, and other outdoor activities.

Zeke often spoke of the exhilarating experiences of those
weeks and the unforgettable impressions the hills made upon
him. Evidently he spent much of his time climbing the
mountains and exploring the rugged terrain. From what he
had seen of the Allegheny Mountains on an occasional visit
to his uncle's home in Pennsylvania and from what he remembered of a trip to the West Coast when he was seven
years old, he was convinced that eventually he wanted to
live in the hills. He came back to Illinois radiant, sun-tanned,
and enthusiastic about life in South Dakota.

"Why does anyone want to live in such flat country as the

Midwest?" he commented. "The hills have real character. When you look up from them at night, you can see so many more stars than you can see from the plains."

The only ominous note that came out of this summer's experience was his mention of the recurrence of double vision. Although we were baffled by the problem, we still did not attach great significance to it; at least we could see nothing urgent.

Part of our attention was diverted from Zeke's physical problem to intensive plans for Jim's wedding in August. Not only were we engrossed in the detailed preparations, but Zeke had been asked by his brother to serve as best man. Since the time between Zeke's return from the Black Hills and the wedding was short, he busied himself in carrying out what was expected of him as best man. However, during a pause at the wedding rehearsal, Zeke, in an aside to his mother, confided that his double vision had gotten worse.

As soon as the wedding was over, we turned our attention undividedly to Zeke's complaint. Since the matter had to do with vision, we naturally turned for aid first to the eye clinic. Repeated trips to the clinic yielded nothing but frustration, as neither new lenses nor special eye therapy afforded relief. Upon recommendation of our family physician, we contacted a prominent neuro-surgeon of Chicago, who put Zeke through a preliminary examination for other possible causes of double vision. The resulting diagnosis read, "Paralysis of the sixth (eye) nerve of unknown origin." Since brain tumor looms large as a possible cause of such neural and muscular aberrations, the surgeon recommended a round of tests in the hospital. Accordingly, he was admitted to a Chicago hospital at once. All of the tests administered at that time, including electroencephalogram, skull x-rays, spinal puncture, and blood sugar tests, yielded negative results. The neuro-surgeon called me. "I can find no cause for his disorder," he said. "I suggest you take Erwin home."

Dissatisfied with the incompleteness of the information gained, I sought the advice of a well-known, older ophthalmologist, also of Chicago, who in a forthright and analytical manner, pointed out several possibilities where such symptoms as Zeke's persist. Admitting that it was impossible at the moment to point with certainty to the trouble, he nevertheless opined that it was one of the following: (1) cyst or tumor; (2) aneurysm; (3) myasthenia; (4) early form of multiple sclerosis.

Presumably the first two of these had been checked out already at the hospital, although, of course, there is always the possibility of error. The third could be checked out at the local eye clinic. (We did this at once with negative results.) Multiple sclerosis is very difficult to diagnose in its early stages, but because the disease is rare in a male of Zeke's age, most medical advice seemed to belittle it as a possibility.

The baffling abnormalcy of his vision plagued Zeke throughout his sophomore year.

As the weeks dragged by with no relief in sight, Zeke urged us to follow the suggestion of another eye specialist who advised an operation on the eye muscles to assist their coordination. Such eye operations were not uncommon and often brought about remarkable results, we were told. Although not all of the physicians we consulted favored the operation before a fixed diagnosis could be established, we nevertheless consented reluctantly to have it done, as Zeke was more than willing to take the risk involved. He kept saying, "It can't hurt anything."

The operation resulted in only temporary relief.

It was late summer and Zeke had already decided to spend his junior year at Westmont College in Santa Barbara, California. Wheaton and Westmont Colleges have a reciprocal arrangement whereby faculty members' children may attend either school with tuition underwritten, and Zeke thought he would take advantage of the opportunity to attend school away from home. I am sure, however, that an important reason for his decision lay in his frustration with life at Wheaton — with the many disappointments he had lately encountered. Perhaps the new setting and environment would help him to get his mind off himself and relieve his problems generally.

When the fall quarter opened, he and I drove to the West Coast in our Pontiac Tempest, which I left with him. After helping him get settled at Westmont, I bade him good-by and turned to leave. A sense of uneasiness engulfed me as I felt keenly his need for support at a time when June and I would be half a continent away. Yet this is what he wanted, and I could do nothing at the moment but trust him to take care of himself.

As I flew back to Wheaton my mind recounted the baffling circumstances which we had all been through. I also thought about the adjustments Zeke would have to make in his new environment, in addition to combating his double vision. As a concerned father, I gave way to worry for a time, but determinedly I committed him to the hands of the faithful Creator.

Save for a few telephone calls and an occasional letter, we had little contact with Zeke between September and Christmas vacation. When he called or wrote, he conversed in a general way — about the friends he was making, and of his impressions of school — but he said little about any physical limitations. However, when he flew home for the Christmas holidays, we noticed new signs of bodily decline.

In the first place, he was wearing a black patch over his right eye. This, he explained, permitted him to see objects singly, as his eyes simply would not coordinate any longer. We could also detect a slow-up in his physical reactions. Of course, we did not call attention to any of these, but he inclined to discuss them now that we were together.

Through Zeke's recounting of his days at Westmont, we learned of his disappointment in try-outs for both baseball and basketball. He had become aware of an alarming ineptitude in baseball and also an inability to dribble a basketball well with his left hand. Also, his sense of balance was impaired. He illustrated his physical slowdown by telling this story. "One day several of us fellows were scrimmaging. I ran down the floor and one of my teammates passed the ball to me near the basket. I broke for the basket and just as I was getting ready for a lay-up a little kid stopped me before I could get the shot away. Several of the fellows laughed at me. I knew I was either terribly out of condition or something was wrong with me." With all of his fortitude and natural optimism, we discerned genuine alarm in his voice. He said he was ready to seek more medical counsel.

Again we sought out our physician, who still belittled the likelihood of anything serious. Detecting the note of desperation in my manner, however, he called the neuro-surgeon whom we had consulted previously and agreed to cooperate with him in administering additional tests and analyses at another Chicago hospital. By this time, Zeke was becoming wary of the doctors' abilities to understand his case. Although he wanted help, he was reluctant to confine himself to the hospital for a new series of fruitless probings — especially when the confinement deprived him of several of his precious vacation days. Nevertheless he consented.

That Zeke's sense of humor had not failed him even under these trying circumstances is illustrated in an interesting sidelight of the tests performed by a local psychiatrist. Our physician knew the case history of Zeke — that he was an athlete and a leader who under the present circumstances might be disturbed psychologically from his inability to perform as in the past. He asked me if I thought Zeke would submit to a psychological test. I said I would ask him.

When I approached Zeke about the matter, he chuckled amusedly and responded, "Sure, it's all right with me, but they are really off base." We, too, were confident that anyone as deliberate, relaxed and well-adjusted as Zeke — who harbored no tensions or unusual frustrations of which we knew, would hardly be plagued with a psychological problem. Nevertheless, the psychiatrist came to his hospital room one day for the test and Zeke submitted to it. Zeke told us the story later. "He was in my room less than ten minutes when he said, 'I see no psychological problems here.'" He laughed as he recounted the steps in the examination. "After asking a few questions the psychiatrist suddenly stopped and let several minutes of silence elapse. I knew he was waiting for me to break the silence, but I decided to wait him out." Zeke again laughed mischievously and continued, "I also knew the first thing he would say after the silence would be, 'What were you thinking about the past few minutes?' When those were the exact words he spoke, I laughed out loud right in the middle of the examination. Immediately afterward, the interview turned into a relaxed, general discussion. Then the psychiatrist left."

By this time what seemed like interminable weeks of fruitless searching and waiting began to take their toll in mounting apprehension and frustration. And probably no emotional suffering is more excruciating than that of prolonged uncertainty. We even began to despair of human help altogether, although we knew that somewhere a diagnosis ought to be available. We began to pray frequently that it might please God to intervene miraculously and at the same time to aid us in our quest for a clear medical diagnosis. On one hand, a person does not want to be guilty of neglect; on the other hand, he does not want to put credence in mere theories that raise false hopes and lead to senseless errors.

As the devil is never tardy in leveling his broadsides against the spirits of God's people, it is hardly surprising that he would single us out for attack now. The devil may concentrate his attacks on the weakest points in the Christian's armor, but he also appears in the well-known guises with which he has had so much success. For example, we heard Satan's voice say, "If you were good, you would be healthy" (which some Christians are ready to buy); also, "If you pray, your trouble is bound to depart" (a striking parallel to Satan saying to our Lord "command that these stones be made bread").[4] We had been tempted before to believe that the Christian always prospers and is exempt from unusual trouble. In numerous ways Satan tried to divert us from seeing God in the adverse circumstances at hand.

Some well-meaning but misguided people are always ready to interpret events. "Sickness," they say, "is punishment by God for sin." Some of my earlier experiences in the ministry had taught me that the puny mind of man lacks the perspective to be sure about God's dealings. In fact, snap judgments may be not only erroneous, but vicious.

While deploring the self-appointed "prophet" who seeks facilely to "justify the ways of God to man," I affirm stongly that belief in Divine Providence affords the Christian an undergirding he can ill afford to lose. To look upon the events of everyday life as merely "routine" is to overlook the reason for existence and to miss the throb of life. God controls men and events. He intervenes to work out His purpose, to chasten, to subdue, or to call to Himself.

Nevertheless, no matter how well-clad one may be with his philosophical armor, he is never fully protected against the shafts that fly from unexpected sources. One fiery dart that pierced my breastplate and proved difficult to dislodge at this early phase of Zeke's illness dealt with the unnaturalness of disease for a man of his age. I had grown accustomed to the normal course of events, to the more regular functioning of the laws of nature. I was used to sunset following sunrise and meridian brightness. The seasons follow each other with predictable regularity. Birds fly north in the spring and return to their southern climes late in autumn. The oak grows tall and mature before decay and death set in. Even though man's allotted years on this earth are three score and ten (so short a span when one computes the age of the world), one presumes he will have time to do the things life usually affords: to enjoy exciting youth, to attend school, to choose a mate, to raise a family, to achieve fulfillment in a life's occupation.

Many times I have shuddered to hear of a baby dying of leukemia or a teenager killed in an auto accident or a young man fatally trapped in a mine shaft. Such untimely happenings contradict so violently the regular cycle of life.

Although I had not yet envisioned the sickness of my son as leading to death, I began to resent its intrusion as unnatural and ill-timed.

I was unable, or unwilling, to see at the moment that all of life consists of both sunlight and shadows.

Shakespeare has said of the body, "in form and moving, how express and admirable"; yet troops of infirmities stand poised to invade it anytime, anywhere without regard for social rank, age, or religious standing.

The immediate results of the laboratory tests revealed no definite source of Zeke's physical disorder. Therefore he went ahead with plans to return to Santa Barbara for the new quarter. When I drove him to the airport, I became painfully aware of his declining physical condition. His impeded balance, unsteady gait, and marked fatigue cast dark shadows over the days to come. Even so, he looked forward to the challenge of the new semester. For the few minutes we had together at the airport, he appeared undaunted by all he had gone through and even spoke excitedly about some of the projects he wanted to accomplish. He mentioned how glad he would be to get back to the warmer climate, to see his good friends, and to resume his studies. He even said he was going to exercise more regularly to get his body in good condition. As he was about to embark on the plane, he flashed me his old mischievous grin.

With a heavy heart I told him good-by. Instinctively, I knew that my boy was being attacked by a monster too deadly for him to cope with.

Soon after I returned home, our physician called for a conference to divulge the most recent information concerning Zeke's diagnosis. I drove immediately to his office.

I had waited but briefly in the auxiliary office when the door opened abruptly and the doctor entered. Without looking in my direction he strode across the room to his desk and sat down. After a moment's hesitation he spoke unemotionally, although his uneasiness and seriousness were unmistakable.

"Probably multiple sclerosis," * he said tersely, without looking directly at me.

The effect of these words on me has already been described.

* "Multiple sclerosis is a disease of the brain and spinal cord caused by an unknown factor that attacks the covering myelin sheath of nerve fibers, causing a temporary interruption of nervous impulses, particularly in pathways concerned with vision, sensation and the use of limbs. . . . A form of allergy may be an important causal factor" (*Encyclopedia Britannica,* Vol. XV, p. 986). More recent information points to a virus as the cause of M.S.

At last I found my voice and asked, "What now?"

"There's really nothing we can do for multiple sclerosis. No one knows what causes it or what can be done when it strikes. Oh, you will find those who are ready to try their theories, but my advice to you is to leave theorizing alone."

Although June and I had been almost frantic to discover the source of our boy's problem, now that I knew, I found little consolation. I believe I understand more fully than before the acute pain of Oedipus, the King, who sought diligently for the truth about himself and at last found that truth to be terrible beyond all description.

My first impulse was to find June and share with her what I knew.

Reaching home and not finding her there, I guessed that she must be at the market, since it was about five o'clock in the evening. Sure enough, I found her in the supermarket parking lot and divulged what the physician had said. Multiple sclerosis sounded vaguely horrible to us, as neither of us knew much about the ways it affected people. The full force of what it implied was yet to come.

"How Long
Do
I Have?"

3.

"How Long Do I Have?"

WHEN INFORMED MEDICAL JUDGMENT avers that your son "probably" has a devastating, unpredictable, incurable disease, do you pass the information along to him?

During his initial round of tests in the Chicago hospital, Zeke saw for the first time other young people with serious neurological disorders. One example was a young man in the same hospital room who was totally blind from a brain tumor, for which he had undergone a series of operations. I remember Zeke turning to me and saying, "Dad, I want you to level with me. If you find out anything from these tests, let me in on it." At the time we were still apprehensive of brain tumor, but I knew then he would want the whole truth, no matter how dire it might be.

Utter honesty and candor had always marked Zeke's life, and I was not inclined to play a role of duplicity with him now. I quickly assured him I would tell him anything I knew. It never occurred to me to consult with the physicians about the advisability of this course of action, but I doubt that their advice would have altered my ultimate decision anyway.

Now that the diagnosis had been made, I found myself hesitating. I had not changed my mind about divulging the facts to him; but the language of the physicians had been guarded and always included the word "probably." That seemed to admit the possibility of error. Since some think multiple sclerosis may be a virus, it sounded much more benign to speak of the problem as some kind of virus rather than risk the specific term with all of its frightening connotations. Why subject our boy to possibly unwarranted worry? At least why not wait until the doctors were sure?

Only a few days after Zeke returned to Westmont College the telephone rang. The voice on the other end of the line was that of a leading neurologist in Santa Barbara who said Zeke had just been in to see him for some shots of acthar. Our local physician had alerted him concerning Zeke's problem, for it was essential to have medical help nearby as the need arose.

The neurologist came quickly to the point. After requesting permission to examine him thoroughly, he asked whether we had told Zeke what he had. When I said we had not because there might be some reasonable doubt, he responded quite emphatically, "I have seen many cases of multiple sclerosis, and that is what he has, beyond any reasonable doubt. Moreover, I believe you ought to tell him at once, for he may overexercise in the gymnasium or over-tax his strength surfing, and such activity militates against the disease. If he is made aware of his problem, he may learn to live within its self-imposed limitations." He also pointed out that later on Zeke might resent our withholding information from him which he was bound to find out anyway.

I remembered how Zeke had said he was going to work out on the rings and bars to get in shape, for he was convinced that lack of physical conditioning could be part of his problem. About a week after my conversation with the neurologist, we received a bill from the local hospital in Santa Barbara for treatment of a deep skull gash from a fall sustained while working out in the gymnasium. My mind was made up. I would tell him at once.

I had never faced a more demanding task than the one then before me. If I could have reached out across the more than two thousand miles and clasped his hand or looked squarely into his eyes and supplied the reassurances to help parry the blow, I might have been partially comforted. But the telephone was the only recourse I had.

About nine o'clock that evening I placed the call. When I got him on the phone, I told him as matter-of-factly as I could what the hospital tests had disclosed. I also spoke of my conversation with the Santa Barbara physician and urged him to submit to an examination.

I waited for Zeke to absorb the content of my disclosure. After a few moments' pause he asked, "Does the neurosurgeon say this?" When I answered in the affirmative, there came another pause. Then his voice broke as he asked, "How long do I have, Dad?"

I could not have winced more from the effect of any physical blow than I did at that moment.

"How long do I have to live?" How does a father answer that question from a boy who has barely passed his twentieth birthday? This is not the type of question I was used to answering for young people. In counseling with students, I have addressed myself to such questions as: What profession shall I pursue? What graduate school shall I attend? Would you advise me to teach, enter the ministry or pursue research? The question before me now was related to death, not life.

Both June and I dropped to our knees immediately to beseech God to give Zeke strength to sustain the blow he had just been dealt. At the time, our telling him seemed such a cruel thing to do. Yet we had no choice, for we knew that Zeke would want it that way. I had also promised to level with him whenever I got a medical confirmation.

Steve Gay said to me later, "I remember the night you called, Dr. Rudolph, and told him the doctors had decided he had multiple sclerosis. . . . For two days it tore him up."

Sleep would not come to our eyes on the long January night as we wrestled with deep darkness of spirit. Throughout the fitful hours we thought of the mental torment which must be our boy's — a torment he must bear alone. We thought of the critical days just ahead as he must make adjustments mentally and socially. Over and over we prayed that God would sustain him miraculously in his hour of need.

That night marked but the first in a long series of sleepless nights when our entreaties for help became increasingly insistent and desperate.

If I were to speak of my initial response to Zeke's trouble as anything but complete discomfiture, I would be less than honest. I have no boasts to make here of fortitude or stoutheartedness. I engaged in no self-heroics. It was as if an antagonist had dealt me a formidable blow in the solar plexus and I had no strength to fight back. My prayers were more like frantic calls for aid than measured affirmations of faith and seeking out God's will. Like one adrift at sea, I saw nothing near on which to cling and all efforts to locate something solid seemed to fail.

Even in this distraught state, however, I can remember harboring no resentment against God in my heart. I felt no inclination to throw God overboard or to deny anything I had believed — to assert an "everlasting no" in the manner of Thomas Carlyle as he declared the meaninglessness of the universe. At the same time, my faith found no resting place.

Something had gone wrong in my own household, and I couldn't see at once what was to be done to rectify it. This may be another way of saying we were in a state of shock and recovery was not immediate. God had not changed. He was still the benevolent, beneficent, holy Being. But at present, we were unable to take hold of Him. The promises of God were still "Yea and Amen!" But in our weakness we couldn't appropriate them.

Even though anguish of spirit under such circumstances is indescribable, as a person recalls the total experience he is aware that special undergirdings of spirit were present at the crucial moments to save him from complete despair. God indeed "knows His own and goes before them." He is the one who also will not allow His children to suffer "above that ye are able; but will with the temptation also make a way to escape, that ye may be able to bear it." [5] "When you pass through the waters I will be with you; and through the rivers, they shall not overflow you; when you walk through fire you shall not be burned, and the flame shall not consume you." [6] "By Him all things consist (cohere)." [7] The word "cohere" suggests that Christ keeps things from coming apart.

How thankful June and I are for the supernatural power which lay beneath all of our anxieties to bear us up on "eagles' wings" just at the moment it appeared we would falter. Whatever God had in mind by letting this experience come was not to be sidetracked easily. In spite of tears, groans, pain, and weakness, we were saved from denial or despair.

In such a state of mind one does not always think clearly or act rationally. His emotional springs are drained; he is unable to deal as objectively with his experiences as at other times. Then it is comforting to realize that God understands our infirmities, our concerns, our burdens, and is touched by them. It is reassuring to know that our Lord is compassionate, loving and kind. Neither is He seeking ways to take advantage of His own. Without claiming unwarranted self-justification, I believe a merciful and understanding God is not unduly censorious of His struggling children who are engulfed in a dark sea of trouble. He wants them to look to Him in adversity, but does not criticize them severely during their initial panic or upset. Of course, He wants them to find at an early point that His "strength is made perfect in weakness." [8]

How patiently God leads!

But what about the mental, physical and spiritual battles ahead for Zeke? Thoughts of him soon displaced our self-preoccupation. The conflict which lay ahead for him was bound to be a formidable one. What would be his response to physical decline? Would he live within the limitations that multiple sclerosis imposed? And how much he needed psychological and spiritual uplift! How would discouragement affect his motivation for study? How would he respond to the prospect of short or impaired life — with increased piety, or with reckless determination to "live it up"? Would he react to events by doubting the goodness of God with resultant bitterness of heart, or would he view his sickness as a molding instrument in God's hands to fashion a deeply spiritual life? How does a young man of twenty think about sickness and possible imminent death? How strong would I be under such circumstances? What interpretation of events could I offer? And how could I reach across the miles to help him in a real way?

Levi Edgecombe, a close friend of Zeke's who was attending Wheaton College, told me, "When I first heard of Zeke's illness I wrote to him immediately, fearing that he might be angry with God, and feeling that I might console him. Was I ever shocked when I received his letter because the entire focus of his reply was on what God had taught him about the meaningful importance of his short life here on earth."

I recall telling my students on numerous occasions when studying the lives of literary figures that it is our response to adversity which counts most and not adversity itself. John Milton, who had suffered the loss of family, property, popularity, and eyesight at a time when he felt his work was only partially done, had grounds for bitterness if he were inclined to interpret events as ordered by a vindictive God. However, he remained subservient to God's will and was mellowed by the years. He stated in the last line of his famed sonnet, "On His Blindness," "They also serve who only stand and wait."

I remember on occasion pointing out both in the pulpit and the classroom that the genius of the Gospel lies not in our always escaping trouble; rather it is that we may have grace to endure when overt deliverance is not forthcoming. Now I was called upon to test the fiber of my faith.

I discovered that the right response to adversity is far from automatic even for the Christian, although he may be determined always to maintain a reverent posture. The tempter is ever on hand to undermine, to cajole, to discourage. The agony of spirit June and I felt at the moment was largely over our fears on Zeke's behalf — for the intense mental pain he must be suffering. We inquired earnestly of God that He would strengthen Zeke's inner life, that He would make up to him what only an infinite and gracious Heavenly Father could supply.

God answered our prayer in a manner "exceeding abundantly above all we could ask or think." In fact, we discovered that even before we had called on Him the answer was already on its way. Subsequent events gave every evidence that Zeke's inner spirit had not flagged.

It may sound strange that one of our early concerns for

our son was that he not withdraw from social life. This came to the forefront of our prayers one evening when two of our close friends from Oak Park, Illinois, were visiting us and sharing our burden. After a time of reading from God's Word we prayed together. I recall June's specific entreaty, "Lord, help him not to withdraw socially. Help him to keep an interest in social life with his friends." She felt this keenly because she knew her son's naturally sociable disposition — how he loved to mingle with others. And if the society of people had been a natural anodyne for him in the past, for him to withdraw to his inner thoughts now could cause him to capitulate to despair.

This prayer evidently pleased the Lord, for it was not long afterward that the telephone rang and Zeke told us of a girl whom he had been dating. From his description we knew he was unusually attracted to her. He said he was anxious for us to meet her. He had never talked that seriously before about a girl.

This was the first time we heard about Claudia ("Corky") Johnson, and her entrance marks one of the most tender and beautiful chapters of his life. No one could convince us other than that God gave him Corky at this crucial period. No other one on earth afforded him as much fellowship, cheer, morale and love as did this unselfish, vivacious, lovable girl. The relationship which began here was to deepen and continue until the end, and was to play an important part in buoying his hopes and sustaining his powers, as well as providing comfort for the lonely hours. The effect was a spiritual one, too, for through her complete commitment to Christ she helped him cast his burdens on God. The author of Proverbs speaks of the price of a virtuous woman as "far above rubies."[9] Certainly the influence of Corky for good was immeasurable.

Later Corky told us of the days when she and Zeke began to date:

He was very casual about everything. He asked me out for the first time in January, 1968. At that time he wasn't very serious either about girls or studying. . . . In the evenings he followed the practice of taking his books to the library ostensibly to study, but he usually spent his time chatting with his friends. After a time he and some of the others would drive out to an eating spot before going home. Whether it was at a restaurant or in the dining hall, Zeke was very nonchalant and his sense of humor kept the other kids in stitches. He was even able to joke about his own awkwardness when he lost his equilibrium and fell. Once on his way to the library he fell and cut his arm on some rocks. In explaining what happened, he said jokingly to some friends, 'Corky and I had a fight. Look what she did to me.'

As time went on, Zeke grew more serious. He seemed more concerned about making good grades. He and I got to going together regularly — about two or three times a week. In fact, after we began to date each other, neither of us went out with anybody else. . . .

It may sound strange, but Zeke and I had gone together for some time before we realized we were from the same section of the country — he from Wheaton, and I from Deerfield, Illinois.

Although Zeke and I had our first date in January, he remarked on several occasions that there was something on his mind he wanted to tell me about very soon. About half-way through March he told me outright that he had multiple sclerosis and that I ought not to get serious with him without realizing what I might be in for. It happened that one of my mother's friends had had the disease for years, so I knew something about it already. I told him I would be the judge of whether I should get involved. But I did admire his honesty about the whole matter. . . .

At this time Zeke was fairly normal in most respects, although he continued to stumble and fall quite often. I noticed the biggest difference in him when we flew home together in June. When we had to walk from one part of the Los Angeles Airport to another and carry our luggage, his strength in his left hand failed. He was very apologetic about being unable to carry a heavy suitcase in each hand. . . .

Naturally, it was still impossible for us to determine the extent of Zeke's depression or just how much he was succumbing to discouragement. We knew there would be low periods, but we were unsure as to just how much spiritual strength he could summon. We wondered whether he would confide in other students and faculty and enlist their prayer support or whether he would choose to keep his malady a secret.

Except for telephone conversations, usually on Sunday nights, news from him was scarce over the next few weeks. He made it clear that he preferred to keep the precise nature of his disease a secret. Although this was hard for him, as well as for us, since it shut away some of the prayer support we needed, we tried to honor his wishes at this point.

However, another problem confronted us as we considered further disclosures. Should not the administration and a limited number of the faculty at Westmont College be apprised of his problem as a safeguard against an emergency? We feared for his well-being if he were to become suddenly ill or incapacitated.

I decided to tell a few key people, but asked each to kindly check on him unobtrusively, without letting him know they had been told. Among those whom I alerted was Zeke's adviser, who is a personal friend and who I knew would be glad to do me a favor. I even informed the president of the college of my solicitude and asked for his help in the event Zeke's condition deteriorated. Both of them reassured me they would do everything in their power to befriend Zeke as the need arose. I am most thankful to these devoted

Christians who responded graciously to my request without betraying Zeke or me. The Christian compassion and selfless concern evidenced by the Westmont administrators and teachers will remain long in my memory. We began to find out that we were the beneficiaries of an innumerable company of people around the country who really cared.

The struggle was only beginning. The uncertainty of the diagnosis was over, but the baffling contest with the disease had just begun. Our quest for spiritual direction was to follow. After the initial shock of the disclosure had worn off, we were to grapple anew with the ruthless strategies of a relentless enemy, Satan. Others had faced similar temptations, some fighting successfully the battle of faith, some succumbing to defeat. But to us no precedent offered aid. Our trial was uniquely our own.

Our spirits were cheered on a few occasions when Zeke called home — often to ask for special help on an English literature assignment. He was an English major, and with our common interest in that field he felt free to enlist my background and experience.

For instance, I remember his calling late one night and saying, "Dad, what do you know about John Donne's poem 'The Dreame'? I realize Donne's metaphysical style gets involved, but this one has me buffaloed. I am supposed to make an analysis of it for one of my English lit assignments. Can you give me some leads right away?"

Just to know that he was even concerned about his studies at this critical point afforded June and me a good deal of relief.

All this time Zeke spoke zestfully of his studies and manifested an interest in earning good marks. For the moment he was winning the battle against defeat. We thanked God for this evidence of courage and strength. At least temporarily Zeke was adjusting to his physical limitations and keeping up his desire to live.

During these trying days, and later, we were to discover some of the stuff of which our boy was made. The resourcefulness and indomitability that began to mark his life were to shine through even under more trying circumstances.

Weakness
and
Strength

4.

Weakness and Strength

PERHAPS THE MOST striking and persistent characteristic of Zeke's illness was weakness — overwhelming, debilitating, devastating physical weakness. Over and over he referred to this mystifying aspect of the disease. Comparing his case with others of whom he had read or had observed in the Multiple Sclerosis Ward at the Northwestern University Clinic, he commented, "None of them seems to be as weak as I am."

And during the weeks of increasing physical weakness and disability, he paradoxically gained in spiritual vitality. This was traceable to a variety of sources.

Zeke had made up his mind to enroll at Wheaton College in September, 1968, principally because he could enjoy some of the solid comforts of home; also he reasoned that he could follow through on the medications he had been trying. However, he dreaded the prospect of trying to keep up a semblance of normality in a place where he was so well-known.

He registered for his courses and actually attended classes

for a few days. But one day when I came home from the college, I found him in the living room discussing with his mother some of the difficulties he had encountered. He was obviously distressed by having to walk up several flights of stairs in the main classroom building, and as he had feared, he felt keenly the nervous strain of trying to walk and converse normally under the scrutiny of well-meaning but over-solicitous friends. He wondered whether it was possible to transfer back to Westmont College immediately. He believed he would be less conspicuous among those who were more familiar with his limitations. I told him he could do whatever he wished.

A quick phone call to Westmont revealed that the dormitories were full but that Zeke was most welcome, if he could find housing. We decided to take our chances and go.

I took off from my classes, and Zeke and I drove to California — this time in a used Chevrolet that we had purchased for him during the summer. When we arrived, Steve Gay opened his apartment to Zeke and even gave up his own bed as a temporary accommodation until other living quarters could be found. I stayed only through the following day before flying back to Illinois.

Zeke was complaining to me of his weakened state, so he and I paid a visit to the local neurologist before I left. I wanted to make sure that the doctor would keep me informed in case of emergency and that he would attend to any physical needs Zeke might have in the days to follow. Dr. Gregg, the neurologist, was most gracious and sympathetic. "You are as near as the telephone," he said to me. But he warned Zeke of over-exertion. "You must take no more than a half load of college work," he advised. "And get lots of rest."

Zeke, with the help of his friends, was able to locate an apartment reasonably close to the college campus.

Late in the fall quarter we received a special delivery letter from the neurologist in California stating that Zeke had been hospitalized for what he and the consulting physician were sure was an attack of influenza. But he said that Zeke was responding favorably to medication and there was no immediate cause for alarm.

Later Zeke told us what had happened on the day he fell ill. Early in the morning he became nauseated, and after protracted periods of vomiting he lost consciousness. Since the other boys in the apartment had gone to classes, no one was available to help him; consequently he lay for several hours alone. Finally he regained semi-consciousness, struggled toward the bed, and pulled himself onto it. He lay there until one of his roommates came home about five hours later. As Zeke was still unable to speak, his alarmed roommate discovered the name of the doctor on a medicine bottle label and called him. Shortly afterward an ambulance arrived and Zeke was taken to the community hospital.

Intravenous feeding and medication helped restore near normalcy in a few hours. He was soon dismissed from the hospital and, though very weak, he was able to go about in much the same manner as he had before. However, as he explained to us later, he seemed to be at the end of his strength at all times. He had no reserve to call upon for even the routine matters which demanded attention. To drive the car to school or to attend classes or to take his meals tired him to the point of exhaustion.

A short time after this occurred, he telephoned us and said, "The doctor has ordered me home for a complete rest, or I must re-enter the hospital at once. I'm coming home." There was no panic in his voice, but he commented that he was experiencing increasing difficulty in getting around and that as soon as he could turn in a couple of papers and take care of whatever final exams he had left he would fly home. Fortunately, the fall quarter was at an end.

Dr. Gregg reported promptly to us Zeke's condition. He said in part:

> Patient seen this morning. He has obviously deteriorated. His gait is markedly unsteady. He is dysarthric even more, is having difficulty swallowing, is still markedly fatigued. I am alarmed about him. This is a significant deterioration. I decided quickly to institute bed rest. The most feasible, realistic way to do this is to have him go home.

Although June and I begged him to buy an airplane ticket outright to come home, even in his weakened condition Zeke insisted on flying standby from Los Angeles to Chicago. He had a mind of his own in these matters, especially when he felt it was extravagant to pay full fare. However, he consented to call us from Los Angeles when his plane was ready to embark for Chicago.

When he emerged from the doorway of the plane and began to dismount the steps to the O'Hare Field runway, he caught sight of us and flashed his inimitable smile. His right hand clutched the rail as he slowly descended the ramp; he had obvious difficulty walking the few yards between him and the terminal. Half-apologetically for his slow, unsteady gait he explained, "I can walk better than this; I'm just stiff from the plane ride."

Knowing Zeke's dislike for open display of emotion, June and I restrained our solicitude as much as possible. Whatever dismay we may have felt for his declining state was at least partially compensated for by the knowledge that now he was near enough for us to minister directly to his needs without the barrier of two thousand miles. Now our hands and feet could lighten his load and provide the rest his body needed.

The Christmas holidays were only a few days away, but

the characteristic fever and zest for gift-buying and celebration were displaced by overriding concerns for Zeke's physical condition. Even the desire to send out the usual Christmas greetings to our friends was lacking. We had planned a trip to our Florida home but were ready to cancel that too, if it became necessary.

The physician advised, however, that while rest was most essential, it did not outweigh a sense of well-being and happiness which might accrue from a trip to the south. The warm climate and new surroundings, together with the society of family and friends, would be good therapy. In fact, the neuro-surgeon in Chicago advised Zeke to follow a course of moderate exercise as long as he did not become over-fatigued.

Zeke looked forward to going south. Not only would it mean a new environment, but it would afford opportunity to spend time with his brother and wife and, most of all, with Corky, who planned to make the trip with us. He stood the automobile trip fairly well, although we decided it would be best for him and Corky to fly back to Chicago after the vacation was over to conserve his limited strength.

Although the Christmas of 1968 was minus the usual hilarity, it was a happy time in a different sense. The few gifts we exchanged with each other seemed to matter very little. Zeke had always opposed buying expensive presents for him. He had said to us, "There's nothing I need or want." But our happiness stemmed from the awareness that for the moment we had each other. In a new way each of us seemed to prize life itself as God's gift. Family ties seemed tighter than usual.

That "hope springs eternal" in the human heart was exemplified during those vacation days in the lives of Zeke and Corky. They had opportunities to go on short walks together and to sit in the sun and talk about their plans for the future. We learned later that it was during this time that they made plans to be married the next fall, if Zeke's condition maintained any kind of stability. If it became necessary for him to live a restricted life, they reasoned that living in the warm Florida climate would be most conducive to his health. Hopes for normal fulfillment bolstered Zeke's spirits greatly and motivated him to fight his disease and to strive to achieve the goals he had set for himself, even though they had to be limited ones.

After the Christmas season was over, Zeke registered for two courses at Wheaton College — one in fiction writing and one in marriage. The writing class met only once a week, but on the fourth floor of Blanchard Hall on Wheaton College campus; the other met on the ground floor of Fischer Hall. For a time he attended these classes. He would drive the car to the door; then he would proceed on his own. We worried about his climbing stairs, but he insisted that no one help him. He attended for a few weeks, but one day he fell in the presence of his classmates and the embarrassment caused him to discontinue the courses.

One of Zeke's high hopes was to become a writer of some sort (he spoke most often of sports journalism). He progressed very well in the fiction writing course until dexterity in his right hand failed. Zeke was primarily interested in the humanities. Samples of his writing exemplify a sensitivity to style and a flair for recreating a dramatic situation.

How does one describe the debilitating weakness which accompanies multiple sclerosis? Zeke said to me many times, "Dad, no one with this disease that I know of has the extreme weakness which I have. No doctor seems to recognize it and call it as such." The doctors frequently spoke of the "fatigue" which accompanied the disease, but that was hardly the same thing.

We who waited on Zeke daily can attest to the intensifying

of the weakness to the point where he was unable to lift his hands to his head, hold a newspaper to read for more than a few seconds or put a fork to his mouth. Weakness — enervating, consuming, terrifying weakness, which made it laborious to place one foot in front of the other or to sit upright without aid on either side or to hold the head upright for long without pillows as support. Weakness, which made it impossible to turn over in bed without assistance — which limited the voice at times to but a whisper.

It was difficult to cope with his complete collapse of strength, but we secured an adjustable tray for reading and a wheel chair for moving about; we also rented a hospital bed which could be raised and lowered for comfort.

Advice from the physician to practice physical therapy proves hollow when no physical strength is available. A physical therapist at the Northwestern University Clinic encouraged us to try gentle exercises in our home, but these were gradually discontinued as strength failed. Daily walks around the block had already been ruled out as too strenuous an activity.

Those who stood by daily and observed the diminishing of strength, the gradual failure of the vital signs, and the lessening of mobility could hardly reconcile themselves to the grim truth that nothing could be done. Although Zeke was not disposed to complain about his daily loss of ground in his combat with the disease, the long, lonely hours were bound to hold discouragement and bleak prospect for him. As I steadied him in his attempts to walk across the room, he would often comment, "I'm getting worse each day." Sometimes the full awareness of his state would descend upon him and he would say, "What is going to become of me?" or "Surely, I must be dying."

Once when I held my arms around him to steady him as he attempted to stand upright, he said, "Dad, what am I going to do?" For the moment my own emotional defenses crumbled. As I held him tightly, I spoke as firmly as I could. "I don't know, son. I can't understand this. I can only say that God sees and understands it all. But be assured that my hands are your hands and my feet your feet. They are yours to use — every minute if you need them. Your mother and I count it a privilege to wait on you."

He seemed to be consoled. Such outbursts of dismay on his part were infrequent. June and I often marveled that he complained as little as he did.

Nevertheless, it was inevitable that his alert, active mind would dwell on his illness and the prospects he faced. He would say at times, "I think about my disease a major portion of the time." More than once he said to me, "I live in a world of M.S."

On April 29, he called me into the living room and said, "Dad, get a pencil and paper and take some dictation. I want to make a list of the things which are wrong with me. The disorders which he enumerated are as follows:

Over-all body weakness — the *major* problem.

Headaches — constant after sleep. Usually relieved by food or Empirin.

Double and blurred vision (paralysis of sixth nerve). Shaking and pulling of eyes. Left eye does not close entirely, causing a fungus on eye during sleep.

Facial numbness — predominantly left side. Facial paralysis in part.

Ringing of ears. Major loss of hearing in left ear.

Dizziness, loss of balance.

Speech slowed, slurred. Strength of voice gone.

Difficulty in swallowing.

Bad taste in mouth.

Tightening in chest.

Left arm, hand extremely weak and almost total loss
of dexterity (total loss coming in the last three
months).

Problem with left leg similar to that of left arm.

Right hand and right leg following slowly the same
pattern of left hand and leg.

Electric shock sensations darting throughout the body.

Cannot walk or feed self without aid. (This has come
in the last few weeks.)

Head throbs when I move.

When a disease can be this devastating, one wonders why
research has progressed so slowly. Though research is by
nature slow and tedious, and recent dramatic achievements
have been made in heart disease, cancer, and Parkinson's
disease, one suspects that we would be much nearer to a
solution of these and other baffling maladies if our national
priorities were properly readjusted. If, for example, we spent
proportionately as much for research as for space exploration,
who can say we might not have achieved breakthroughs
where we still must bemoan our helplessness?

A heart-rending illustration of the spirit being willing but
the flesh weak came one evening when he said to me, "Dad,
in the past I have let you do most of the praying when we
were together. I have said I would not pray merely to be
heard by some other person or to give the impression of re-
ligiosity. Now I believe I can pray with you in sincerity."

He was sitting in his wheelchair at the time and I wheeled
him to the open door facing our backyard and stood behind
him, letting his head lean back against my body for support.
June stood by my side as we listened intently to the words
of that prayer. He spoke deliberately, beginning with thanks-
giving for what God had wrought in his life, giving thanks
in particular for the lessons he had learned. In a short time

his words diminished to a whisper. The last words we could make out had to do with his thankfulness for those who cared for him. When strength failed altogether, I said, "Amen," and stood silently for several minutes, still steadying his head as he leaned against me.

Even in the face of a downward trend physically, Zeke did not give up hope. He had read of many cases of the disease that had reversed their course and tried to find out what they had done to bring about the change.

We heard through a friend of a doctor in the West who had achieved success with several patients through a fat-free diet. We sent for his books and even talked with him on the phone. He sounded hopeful — particularly if one followed the diet scrupulously in the early stages of the sickness. One lady wrote that she had experienced remarkable results from the diet — rising from a bedfast condition to a state of near normalcy, even to resuming her duties as a church organist.

Zeke agreed to follow the diet faithfully. He had nothing to lose, even if the theory were unfounded. His mother deserves all the credit for faithfully preparing his meals with the right balance of fats and proteins and serving them to him punctually, with a supplement of vitamins. Although the diet accomplished little that we could see, June did not deviate a hair's breadth for many weeks from the rigorous outline prescribed. And Zeke cooperated admirably in the experiment.

Although weakness was predominant during the months of declining health, in an extraordinary way we witnessed in Zeke a paradoxical display of strength. The strength, of course, was that of a courageous heart fighting back, keeping up zest for life. It was the will to plan for the future, refusing to think of the present as anything but a temporary impairment, which through sudden natural reversal or divine intervention would pass away. It was the strength of a spirit which was fed from an inexhaustible source.

Much of the resource for this strength lay in Zeke himself. Evidence of this was revealed in his remarkable ability to adjust to new physical setbacks as they occurred. When his mobility became impaired, he spoke appreciatively of being able to carry on even a semi-normal life. As the disease attacked one member of his body, and then another, he emphasized his gratitude for those parts yet unaffected. When he could no longer move about, he said optimistically, "My eyes still work; I can read. And my mind is good." In the midst of insufferable discouragement he was able to see compensations and remaining signs of hope.

There were also reservoirs of strength around Zeke which afforded their soul-sustaining comfort. One of the supplies of his inner strength was reading. No longer able to attend class on campus, he turned to reading at home. He began to read Shakespeare's plays. He said, "If I can't write, I can become an authority on Shakespeare." Interest also grew in systematic reading of the Bible. Usually the morning hours from nine to eleven-thirty were his best for reading. After breakfast he would get comfortably situated in his chair, with his pillow behind his head and the reading tray adjusted to the proper height and read and munch on jujy-fruit candy until exhaustion overcame him.

Quite regularly, especially in early evening, Zeke liked to talk about things he had been reading or thoughts that had lately come to his mind. I would sit on the sofa opposite him and listen to his reflections and respond to some question he might raise. We conversed about many things. Usually they were serious topics including problems of today's youth, unrest on college campuses, modern music, the generation gap. Or we would discuss the meaning of a passage from the Bible or explore the implication of a passage from literature.

It was during some of these conversations that I became acquainted with my son in depth. I had never before encountered in him such maturity of insight. I know now what some of his close friends meant when they spoke of the striking manifestations of seriousness in his last weeks.

Berry Fiess, Zeke's next door friend, recalls the following:

> I found out about the exact nature of Zeke's disease on a fishing trip we took to Wisconsin in September, 1968. Here is the way it happened: When I came back from my first army school training, I went over to see him to talk over old times and he suggested that we go fishing. Although his parents weren't much in favor of the idea — considering the way he felt, he insisted that he was a good judge of what he could do, so we packed our gear, piled into my VW and set off.
>
> We had not gone far from home when Zeke became very serious and said, "Berry, I want to tell you something." I must have indicated surprise as I looked at him and answered, "Yes?" "I have a funny disease," he went on. "That's the reason I have to wear this patch over my eye." "Didn't the ophthalmologist find the trouble?" I asked, trying not to show my emotion openly. "No," he replied. "It's something else that they don't really have a cure for."
>
> I admired his tremendous frankness and courage. He spoke even then and later of the hope he had for getting better. Even with such a weight upon his heart, he was extremely cheerful during the entire trip. When he stumbled, he would pick himself up and go on as though nothing unusual had happened. One time as we were getting out of the boat, he slipped and fell into the water. After he fell, he just looked up and laughed.
>
> Our fishing expedition was not very successful, although we tried repeatedly several places where others said they were biting. Zeke had quite a few fish stories to tell of other times when he had caught them, but all we got on this trip was a sun-tan. Of course, we offered our excuses, as most fishermen do.

Again Berry wrote, "In February, 1969, when I was home on leave from the army, I was able to see Zeke again. Inside, he was truly a most remarkable person . . . . When he used to walk around the block each day, I liked to go with him occasionally and talk with him. . . . It was at this time I noticed Zeke's mind had matured abnormally fast. I felt like a child next to him. . . ."

Here is an excerpt from a letter dictated by Zeke to Corky and sent to Berry May 23, 1969, when he was in Taiwan:

> It's quite a coincidence, but I've been reading a lot about Paul myself. He seems to have a lot of good things to say about trusting in Christ and a real faith, which we both seem to need at this time. I must admit my faith has really been tested by the slackening of my condition. Certain people, like yourself, and relatives and friends, especially Corky, have shown me what it's like to have real friends in times of need. I can't believe how many people have been praying for me and it really means a lot to me.
>
> Whether I get better or not is out of my hands, but I have a feeling that God still has a purpose for me somewhere.

He understood today's youth better than I. He could identify with their sense of alienation, their frustration and shared their antipathy for sham and hyprocrisy. He was quick to tell me of the points where I failed to understand them and where my biases were apparent. If I manifested impatience with a student who did not see eye to eye with my generation, he would say, "Dad, you've stopped listening; you have shut your mind off and are talking from pure prejudice." He made me stop and analyze my actions and the motives behind them.

One day we talked at length about modern music. Zeke's stereo-record library represented a wide variety of modern styles, as well as the more traditional ones. He pointed out the great influence which such groups as the Beatles had upon modern young people. He observed, "The Beatles had a great opportunity to lead young people in the right direction, for with all of their novelty and experimentation they were seeking a satisfying way of life." He commented further on how they drew many young people after them when they sought out the mystical religion of India and then dashed the hopes of the youth by rejecting God and the supernatural. "Such albums as 'Magical Mystery Tour' and 'Sergeant Pepper's Lonely Hearts' Club' and the later Beatles' reference to the man who believed God to be 'the fool on the hill' depict this rejection," he said.

Frequently we talked about modern man's value system. Zeke scorned the materialism and pleasure seeking of today's average professing Christian. He said, "Social ties and pleasure-laden activities within the church have displaced the message of the supernatural and the separated life."

To hear such seasoned comment coming from one so young in years was unusual, although there had always been a latent tendency in him to minimize material concerns. He had remarked even before he became ill that in order for modern man to realize his life's potential he must look beyond bigger cars, homes, financial security, or luxuries. He spoke of "spoon-fed" youth spoiled by "a materialistic but soul-deadened society" as searching for ultimate values and trying to find meaning. He pointed out that in his judgment, ninety percent of groups such as radical college students, hippies, "flower-children," and runaways were made up of youth who were merely discontented with the emptiness of their existences. [*]

During these serious talks I could not fail to note the

---

[*] Some of Zeke's reflections on these and other subjects appear in the texts of his papers written in the weeks prior to his death and are given in full in a later chapter. He also took a literature course and courses in Christian doctrine which point to the vitalization of his inner powers as physical strength failed.

honest, straightforward comments he made about himself and others.

The days of Zeke's confinement were brightened by frequent visits from his brother Jim. Even though there was seven years difference in their ages, which in the past had been the grounds for differing interests and points of view, Zeke always looked up to Jim. He saw in Jim the epitome of self-discipline which he at times had lacked. Some of his most endearing words during his last days were reserved for his brother.

Being sports-minded, both of them found common ground in talk about their favorite competitions. Both were adept at living-room quarterbacking or evaluating the merits of a sports hero.

Just to have Jim nearby seemed to strengthen Zeke greatly. He welcomed and needed someone near his age with whom he could share his burden. The attachment of brother to brother afforded Zeke much-needed soul sustenance and drew them together in the fellowship of suffering which, I am confident, has made an indelible impression on Jim's life as well. Indeed the extent Zeke's illness and early death have affected his brother is immeasurable.

Much of the time Zeke preferred to conceal the full story of his sickness from his friends. But it was natural to tell Jim all about it. Not infrequently Jim would lift him into his car and take him for a short ride into the country. Despite the fatigue that resulted, he came back refreshed in spirit.

Many times I entered into conversations with the two boys; more often I would leave them to converse alone. Occasionally I would hear laughter coming from their direction, which was far more healing for Zeke than any doctor's prescription.

Another great source of strength to Zeke was Chaplain

Evan Welsh of Wheaton College whose visits were like gentle zephyrs from heaven. His stays were sudden and brief, but warm. Possessed with authentic Christian concern, this man of God in his characteristically buoyant manner took special interest in whatever Zeke might be doing, chatted briefly, prayed, spoke a few words of encouragement, and was on his way. Once I heard Zeke say after Dr. Welsh was gone, "That was good." The Chaplain's visits seemed to lift more than to tax Zeke's strength. It was natural for him to turn to this godly man for spiritual counsel.

But of all the sources of strength available to Zeke, none bore him up "on eagles' wings" more than the week-end visits of Corky. Enrolled in her junior year at Northern Illinois University, she made it her regular practice, as studies and other commitments permitted, to spend the weekends at our house to be near Zeke. Although it pained him to give her the impression that he was anything like an invalid, he nevertheless looked forward to her visits and confided in her freely as she shared her understanding and concern. Her abounding vitality and cheerful, optimistic manner were a healthful tonic to his quailing spirit. "But I can't do that, Corky," he would say as she urged him to try to walk. "Oh, yes, you can," was her cheery rejoinder, and he would try again.

Once when I approached Corky with the subject of Zeke's impairment and discouraging outlook, she said, "Zeke and I are praying that if God wills, he will get better. Of course, when we see no improvement, each of us begins to wonder what will happen to us. Such as this has been known to go on for years. I realize that he might be bedridden indefinitely, and that would be a problem for both of us. However, we have decided to trust the Lord for each day."

As long as Zeke was able they took short walks together;

again, they would play the stereo or watch a program on T.V. or just talk. June and I witnessed with joy their complete contentment in each other's company — the way their faces would light up as they became engrossed with each other, or gave vent to spontaneous laughter. Love between them deepened rapidly.

One final boon to Zeke's spirits came in July when our family decided to take a trip to Bradford, Pennsylvania, to visit Zeke's uncle and aunt, who were perennial favorites of his, largely because of their capacity for fun. They were also dedicated Christians and had two sons approximately the same ages as our own. Through the years, because we had interests in common, we took numerous vacations together boating and water skiing.

We were happily surprised when Zeke consented to make the trip east, for his suffering during recent weeks had been more intense than usual. At the time, we wondered about the advisability of such a trip, but he expressed an eagerness to go. June fixed him a bed in the back seat of the car, and he stood the trip without unduly adverse effects.

Bradford, Pennsylvania is a delightful spot; in many ways it is the perfect resort area — especially in the summer. Zeke's uncle's home is away from the noise of city streets, nestled at the foot of one of the wooded hills where one may breathe deeply the pine-scented air and listen to the babble of the spring-fed brook as its shallow waters tread over the stones. Rising abruptly above the water, the foothills of the Allegheny Mountains, with their dense growth of pine, cedar, and oak, extend far away.

One can naturally say in such a setting, "I will lift up mine eyes unto the hills, from whence cometh my help." Indeed, the hills already had begun to beckon Zeke to come away. Little did we realize that the day was so near that he would heed their summons.

Gentle but strong hands lifted Zeke in the wheelchair each evening to the shelter-house adjoining the brook, where he would sit and watch the playful waves and feel the caress of the refreshing breeze. One of us would usually sit by him for long periods — without saying a word, unless he chose to break the silence. Nature, with her many voices, may already have been inviting him to come away with her from the pain and heaviness of earth. I could not hear those voices, for I did not stand on the vantage point to hear celestial sounds as did he. Only a few miles from this very spot, within less than a fortnight, he was to take his place in waiting for the Resurrection.

The
Face of
Adversity

5.
The Face of Adversity

As a rule, in cases such as Zeke's the physical pain and disability are outmatched by the mental turmoil, anxiety, and inner suffering which accompany them. I can easily see how such a state in the life of a non-Christian could produce deep distress and frustration — even despair. However, God seemed to mitigate Zeke's inner stress and bring about a general tranquillity of spirit which was broken only by an occasional lapse into discouragement as he saw new signs of physical deterioration.

The five emotional stages through which the very ill proceed as described in the Ross study did not coincide with the emotional pattern through which Zeke passed, although some correspondence of those reactions appeared intermittently. ° The first stage — that of denial — did occur for a

° Dr. Elizabeth Kubler-Ross, *Life* magazine, Nov. 21, 1969, in a study of people who face imminent death, said that these people pass through five emotional stages along the way of death. They are (1) denial, when the patient refuses to accept his real predicament; (2) anger — with the doctor or his own family or both; (3) bargaining, in which the patient bargains for an extension of time, with promises to lead a life dedicated to God and other useful purposes; (4) depression, grief; (5) acceptance.

time, but that was during the long exploratory search for a diagnosis. When multiple sclerosis was suggested as a live option, Zeke invariably refused to consider it. However, as soon as the medical authorities agreed upon the diagnosis, he did not openly discredit it. This is not to say that he never wondered whether the doctors understood his case entirely, for on numerous occasions, when his disease appeared to develop so rapidly, he wondered whether there might be a tumor, or some other obstruction yet undiscovered, which was interfering additionally with his neurological responses.

I don't recall that anger comprised a definite stage of Zeke's illness. There were times when he would fling his glasses from him in exasperation as he tried to read the newspaper or hold a book upright; I remember his saying on one occasion as he looked into the mirror and noted his reddened complexion caused by the cortisone, "I wonder what God wants with me like this." Only once did I hear him say disconsolately as he experienced difficulty walking across the living room, "Only twenty-one, and look at me!" But such reactions were occasional and exceptional rather than characteristic. I was amazed that he restrained himself as well as he did. And he never blamed us or the doctors, except to regret that medical science knew so little about his disease.

Zeke never bargained with God that I knew of, though I could hardly know all that passed through his mind during his days on the West Coast, or even in his silences at home, for that matter. That he underwent a significant deepening of his religious experience only a few weeks after receiving the official diagnosis pointed to intimate dealings between himself and God. He said in a telephone conversation with us, "If I can have twenty more years of life, I will be satisfied." But that sounds like an adjustment to the urgency of the moment more than striking a bargain. I recall that he revised the number of years he hoped for to ten, then five, as he faced the increasingly grim prospect of the future. His remarkable ability to adjust to the changing situation kept his hopes alive. He would even say on occasion, "Sometimes I wonder whether this disease might run its course and I will regain my health."

The fourth stage of the Ross report was uncharacteristic of Zeke. He seldom gave way to depression. The clear words of Paul were demonstrated in his outlook, "cast down, but not destroyed." [10] Zeke accepted his disease readily. I believe he also accepted readily the possibility of dying at an early age, although thoughts of this kind were punctuated with hopes that he might yet recover.

Multiple sclerosis is a mystifying disease. One can seldom find two people in whom its course runs parallel. Sometimes people experience an exacerbation and then continue on a plateau for years before experiencing another. Treatment by acthar or cortisone during one of these attacks may produce temporary respite.

Attacks vary in severity and resulting disability, as well as in frequency. In some instances, the patient may experience a complete reversal of disability. We have already mentioned that one woman in a western state who read about Zeke wrote us saying that after adhering to a diet prescribed for her by a doctor in Oregon she arose from a bedfast condition to resume her normal duties. Other dramatic instances of reversals in the course of the disease were related to us by people whom we met, and these precedents gave rise to hope that the same thing might happen again. The most common trend of the disease, however, is downward, with periodic plateaus of the *status quo*.

No matter how much we may speak of acceptance of death or spiritual serenity in the face of adversity, no one, except the person caught in the throes of a terminal disease, can

properly attest to the perturbation and anguish of spirit.
Only the Lord and Zeke know what went on inside of him
during the long hours when he sat alone and contemplated
his prospect. From experience I know that Satan attacks
one relentlessly when he has an advantage. When Zeke told
me, "I live in a world of m.s." and "I think about my disease
most of the time," I knew something of the clouds of deep
concern and dismay which had darkened his outlook. He
also said on several occasions, "I would rather die than continue like this."

A letter to his brother Jim, written November 22, 1968,
shortly before he was ordered home for complete rest, de-
scribes some of his state of mind:

Dear Jim and Dotty,

Well I guess I finally did get around to writing. It's
funny how much I think about you people and how seldom
I write. This quarter, with the doctor holding me down to
only two courses, it's amazing how much time I've had just
to think and be by myself. It pays in loneliness at times,
but I think I've adjusted a great deal, and gotten my values
a bit straightened out.

The kids out here are just great to me. I know now I
made the only sensible move, as I couldn't have taken the
weather and emotional strain back there. I miss many things
about Wheaton, but that life is slowly becoming just the
past. I know now I'll have to settle out here to stay at all
mobile. I really hope this doesn't mean that we will always
be this far apart. Maybe in time I can convince you as to
the merits of Santa Barbara. (Have you seen the snapshots
Dad took?)

That really sounds great about your going to Europe. It
should really be an experience and it sounds like you're
hitting all the right places. Next in line will be a trip to
the West Coast.

By the way, it was 80 degrees and clear today (humidity
12%), with a 15-mile-per-hour off-shore breeze. Maybe tomorrow it will be nice! I spent about an hour and a half

today at a cliff lookout place I like over the ocean. Whenever I feel low or have no strength, I go there and it seems to pick me up. It's strange when you become limited. You really have as much fun. It's just that simple things, relationships, and beauty become much more real and enjoyable. That's the truth.

Well all I can say is I'm really looking forward to seeing you and talking with you. I haven't been feeling well lately, so I may be home about the 8th instead of the 11th. I guess I'll be there when I get there. Keep your casting arm loose!

Love,
Zeke

While I could never fully fathom the extent of Zeke's inner sufferings, I know well my own pain and mental disquietude. Many questions arose with new intensity. Annoying problems have a way of persisting in adversity, even when one thinks he knows some of the correct answers. Often one discovers that seemingly simple questions probe great mysteries and elicit complicated replies.

One stubborn question was, how does one pray in a circumstance of this kind? Does he consider disease as an intrusion upon God's will and demand unequivocally that God remove the trouble? My whole training and inclination dictated that I pray for God's will to be done, and that if it be His will to heal, then for this to be accomplished.

Of course, the manner of accomplishment, as well as its timing, must be left to God, I had been told. But as I prayed now, my inclination was to ask God to heal speedily.

I recall some Christians advising us to pray otherwise — that the "if" clause which we prefaced to our prayer (if it be Thy will) was an equivocation to cover our paucity of faith. "The kingdom of heaven suffereth violence, and the violent take it by force," [11] they pointed out.

These conflicting views disturbed us. On one hand, we

did not want to fail on the point of believing; neither did we want to offend an omniscient God by insisting on our own way.

Then there was the question, how long does one persist in prayer? Is prayer for healing asking a reluctant God to do something He is disinclined to do? Must one overcome God's reluctance by importunity? Or must we exercise the discipline of prayer to accomplish on our part a state of readiness or preparation where faith can subsist? Must we ask and keep on asking, even as we are enjoined "Ask . . . seek . . . knock"? Or must we seek a place where faith rests in quiet trust and confidence? Such a course appeared logical, but it assumed a daring stance of spiritual confidence which risked falling short if God meant to continue lessons for us in disciplined prayer.

Also, there was the question of united prayer. How necessary is it to enlist others in the common purpose of prayer? If "the effectual fervent prayer of a righteous man availeth much," [12] do the effectual, fervent prayers of many avail much more? Or if one righteous man is righteous enough, does his faith remove all mountains? I recall righteous Abraham's prayer for Lot, which was accomplished single-handed, with importunity. Jesus Himself enjoined upon His disciples the need for faith — that if faith were as a mustard seed, mountains would be removed. [13] However, one notes other illustrations in the Bible of the view that strength comes through united prayer: David commented that when he went into the house of the Lord (where other saints were), then he understood some things which had baffled him before. [14] Also, a group of early-church Christians were praying unitedly when Peter's chains fell off and he walked out of prison. [15] The disciples were all of one accord in one place in an attitude of united prayer when the Holy Spirit descended and the era of Pentecostal fullness was ushered in. [16] Our Lord also taught that "where two or three are gathered together in my name, there am I in the midst of them." [17]

I do not think we ever found a satisfactory answer to the question of united prayer. Always before us lay the challenge to believe. "Said I not unto thee, that, if thou wouldst believe, thou shouldst see the glory of God?" [18] We searched our hearts to discover impediments to faith.

Speaking conservatively, I would estimate that thousands of people over the country became involved in intercessory prayer on Zeke's behalf: people in the church where we attend, other individual congregations from far and near, faculty and staff at Westmont and Wheaton Colleges, colleagues in June's and my profession from various schools, Billy Graham Association members, people whom we had never met, but who had heard of Zeke's affliction and who shared their concern. I am indebted particularly to the students and faculty of Wheaton College. Until this day a student will stop by my office or drop a note via college post office or write from a distance to give reassurance and promise of continued prayer. It is not unusual for a concerned colleague to reach out his hand of sympathy and compassion to ease the pain he knows is deep and persistent.

The fact that God prompted so many people to pray causes me to believe that the faith exercised did not go unnoticed. Some of the conclusions arrived at in these pages stress the point that God did hear the prayers of His people.

The supernatural undergirding of Zeke's spirit during his days of trial, as well as June's and my own hopeful outlook, are traceable only to the grace of One "who is touched with the feelings of our infirmities" and whose strength is "made perfect in weakness."

When at first we were reticent to make general appeals for prayer, one of my colleagues reasoned with me that we were unwise to cut ourselves off from the resource of united prayer. He recalled how in the past God had miraculously intervened when the college family had prayed concertedly. After a short deliberation, we heeded his advice and laid our petition before others who joined us gladly at the throne of grace. Some of our encouragement came from the house of prayer where large groups were engaged in intercession; however, many of our precious recollections are of moments spent in prayer and meditation with a few close friends whose faith in God was unshrinking.

From what I could ascertain, there was no consensus on the part of those who prayed as to whether Zeke would be healed. A few felt confident he would be; none that I know of thought he would not be. Most were non-committal. God's will seemed inscrutable, although the Spirit's presence was pronounced wherever prayer was offered in his behalf.

Whenever physical conditions remain unchanged in the face of prayer, one begins to cast about for possible explanations. At least that was my inclination, although I really had no business doing it as much as I did. Was the illness to teach the victim and those around him some abiding lessons in faith? Was it God's purpose to refine the quality of His children in the furnace of affliction? Even more penetrating, was God doing this because I was out of His will? Could my own disobedience cause God to raise a red flare of warning by touching one of my own? Or could it be that God foresaw that Zeke might not live for Christ if his life were to continue indefinitely and decided to take him away early? What would one give to hear God speak audibly on these points! One queries with Henry Vaughan, a seventeenth-century poet:

> O Father of eternal life
> And all created glories under Thee,
> Resume thy spirit in this world of thrall
> Into true liberty.

Either disperse these mists which blot and fill
My perspective still as they pass,
Or else remove me hence unto that hill
Where I shall need no glass.[19]

Zeke questioned many times whether God might be realizing a purpose through his affliction. He was saved from bitterness, I am sure, by assuming that a kind and loving God would deal no hardships without envisioning a gracious or noble end. Zeke's friend, Steve Gay, had underlined Zeke's recognizing M.S. as a means for bringing him to his senses. The letter Zeke wrote to Berry Fiess who was in the armed forces abroad, in May, 1969, bore on this point: "If I've ever had a good influence on you or still can, that will be serving a purpose. I must admit I sit and wonder about what the reasons are for my illness, but if I can help other people in this way, at least that will still be serving a purpose."

As has been intimated already, ascertaining God's purpose is enigmatic, if not hazardous. And in the end, one must rely on a Person rather than decipher events. At least, one knows that happenings in the Christian's life are more than blind chance. The nearer one gets to God the more he is caught up in the awe and the glory of what God is doing.

Being of a naturally independent nature, Zeke desired at first to conceal the details of his illness from all but a few intimate friends. We were sensitive to his wishes for a time, but soon it became evident that little was to be gained by secrecy. Furthermore, general requests for prayer made it virtually impossible to avoid specific reference to the nature and seriousness of the disease.

From the outset, June and I were as much concerned with his psychological reaction as with the threat of new physical inroads made by the disease. We talked regularly with him by long-distance telephone, but we could not always be sure whether he was in good spirits for our sakes or whether he really possessed a sense of well-being. Seldom did he convey discouragement, except to let us know in a general way about new-occurring symptoms, such as loss of balance or excessive fatigue.

Knowing of the threatening nature of multiple sclerosis, June and I were driven to extremity in our fears for him — especially since we felt so helpless and far away. Sometimes when we thought of the possibility of blindness or deafness, mental derangement, or loss of speech, which sometimes occur in the advanced stages of the disease, we became almost inconsolable.

However, I remember a prayer we made almost desperately during those days, which God was pleased to honor. We asked God in mercy to grant Zeke as a least common denominator the following benefits: first, that his mind remain unaffected; second, that he not be deprived of eyesight; third, that he not lose his hearing completely; and fourth, that he retain his ability to speak. God, in mercy, heard our anguished cries. In the end, Zeke never lost these faculties, and he retained the normal use of his mental powers. How good God is, even in adversity.

Some of the questions Satan brings during adversity contain more than a modicum of plausibility. The prophet Habakkuk warns us of this when he asks why such a cruel and violent people as the Chaldeans were permitted to overrun the Jewish nation, which was much more righteous than the Chaldeans. How long would God forbear without interfering and protecting the innocent? I believe Habakkuk really knew the answers to his questions when he raised them, but Satan succeeds well in interjecting doubts into the minds of God's people when the righteous continue to suffer for no apparent reason. However, Habakkuk at last broke through into the sunlight of God's presence and affirmed with renewed conviction, "the just shall live by faith" and "the Lord is in His holy temple." As with Habakkuk, so with us; the confrontation with doubt is real and the struggle intense.

For a time the question "why?" did not press hard upon me. As long as Zeke's affliction was not acute and hope for at least a physical stalemate was imminent, the word "why?" lurked only on the rim of my thoughts. I knew that the Christian was not exempt from suffering, that the rain fell on the just and the unjust, that life was made up of both pleasure and pain. But as the days of sorrow lengthened, I found God's ways more baffling and tantalizingly inscrutable.

The tincture in the question continued to be the unnaturalness of it all. Zeke had prepared for life, not death. He stood on the threshold of promise and fulfillment, not denial and oblivion. Why was our son permitted to live normally up to a point, then be cut off suddenly? The abnormality was further compounded by the fact that this was a rare disease; not more than one in fifty thousand is afflicted with it. Had not God said, "No plague shall come nigh thy dwelling?" Of all accidents, why this untimely marauder, multiple sclerosis?

In Dostoyevsky's *Brothers Karamazov*, Ivan, the intellectual, stated that while he accepted God as a fact, he nevertheless refused to accept the world God had made. He gave as one of his reasons the fact that God allowed violence and bloodshed in His world — even the murder of innocent children. Ivan was not the first, nor the last, to wrestle with this imponderable. And there are others: Why do the godly suffer? Why do the wicked prosper? Why are the righteous cut off? Why do innocent people undergo loss of home, lands, and life itself? Or why does death come uninvited to those who are young in years?

A person may suppose he has framed the answer to the age-old question, "Why?" but when he is personally involved in trouble, he can only find peace when, like Thomas, he places his hands in the wounded side of our Lord and utters, "My Lord and my God."

Through it all, June's and my overriding concern was that Zeke enjoy a more glowing religious experience. He had never been a rebellious sort, though his Christian testimony was most pronounced during his high school days when he attended youth meetings regularly in the local church. College tends to be a severe period of tumult, testing, critical thinking and adjustment of perspectives, and for Zeke it was no exception. Our prayers concentrated most earnestly on the point that Zeke not grow bitter or resentful about what was happening to him. We were confident that the Lord had something better for him spiritually, and we did not want him to miss it.

Naturally, June and I continued to wonder whether we could do more for him medically. Although we tried to keep abreast with research on multiple sclerosis and were in constant touch with the Northwestern University M.S. Center, we were often tempted to try distant medical centers of renown, such as those in Rochester and Baltimore. But finally we knew that human hands were not enough.

We often prayed that Zeke would not resent being dependent on us. And we feared that his independent nature might react adversely against our inevitable solicitude. We hoped that we might in no way abort his sense of manhood and determined to share his burdens as unobtrusively as possible. We were soon to learn that Zeke was heroic in battle and able to look well beyond anything we had thought possible.

A Turning Point

6.

A Turning Point

WE BECAME AWARE of a marked change in Zeke's spiritual outlook when he came home from Santa Barbara at the end of the fall quarter in 1968. He was more inclined to discuss spiritual subjects, and the greater vitality of his Christian life and outlook was manifest in numerous ways. He even said to me, "I'm different from what I was."

One could not help noticing his increased sensitivity to spiritual values and determination to make his life count for God through Christian witness. His concern for the church and compassion for other people were revealed in his manner. He discounted the value of earthly possessions and relished the simple joys and solid realities of life. We noticed these modifications of character, but guessed that they must be the result of the intense inner struggle through which he had been passing. Zeke did not give us the details of what occurred on campus to help him get his spiritual bearings. It was not until Steve Gay, Zeke's closest friend at Westmont, came east that I heard the full story of what was back of the change.

Steve called me aside on the day Zeke was buried. He asked, "Did Zeke ever tell you about the real turning point in his life — and mine?" I answered, "He told us how his outlook upon life had been much affected by some prayer meetings held by a group of fellows at Westmont; however, he never filled us in on all of the details."

As Steve and I strolled along the spring-fed brook in northern Pennsylvania, he told me the story of several unusual meetings which had produced marked changes in the lives of several young men — and of one meeting in particular. Read his own account as he related it to me on that August afternoon in the rustic solitude and quietness of the Allegheny foothills. I am reconstructing it as near verbatim as I can: *

> I do not remember the exact moment I met Zeke, but I remember well my first impression of him — the way he moved, the dark patch over his eye, his laugh. The talk was that he was a fairly good pitcher and from Wheaton, Illinois. . . . A couple of times while playing soccer I saw him running and noticed that he had apparent difficulty in making his body react, but thought nothing of it at the moment. Then one night we played basketball together and he complained of his poor shooting. I could see that at one time he had been good, but that now his reflexes were too slow for him to be a good ball player. It was at this time that I got to know him a little better.
>
> As our friendship deepened, we would go out on dates together and goof off. Once in a while we would talk about matters a bit more serious. Sometimes we would play cards together, for Zeke liked anything that was competitive. His emotions were written all over his face. He would smile broadly when he got good cards and manifest displeasure

* Steve confirmed the details of the story in a letter which he wrote me later.

when his hand was poor. It was about this time also that Zeke would lose his balance occasionally and fall off chairs, into closets, or anywhere. Everyone would howl with laughter when this happened, Zeke included. Of course, none of us suspected anything seriously wrong with him.

Then one night you called, Dr. Rudolph, and told him that the doctors had decided he had multiple sclerosis, and for two days it tore him up. We spent one whole night awake talking, and then we were quiet for awhile. Nothing spiritual was talked about then, but I felt that it was a terrible thing and that I was a most fortunate person to have good health.

Then it began to hit me. If this were possibly for a purpose, then everything would turn out all right. Later on while we were goofing around in my room and Zeke and I were laughing, suddenly a weird, deep remorse came over both of us. He broke down into tears and asked out loud why God had been so unkind. With much more bitter emotion and tears I privately cursed God for ever doing something like this.

It happened about that time that a group of the guys, mostly athletes who were not enjoying church-going, were talking among themselves about their dissatisfaction with the contemporary church and Christianity in general. Out of this came a small group of guys who decided to meet every Sunday morning informally to discuss anything that came into their minds. These men were not well-known for their association with Christ.

Slowly, a change began to take place. It was hard to pinpoint exactly what it was, but a genuine love and concern began to grow. John S., Steve C., Zeke, and I were the closest in the group. Tom D., Dave L., Carl C., and others joined later on.

Well into the fall quarter, a group of seven men in professional positions came to Westmont campus to speak for a week. They were all committed Christians and excited about God as a result of close fellowship in their "CORE" group. Lambert Dolphin, a top nuclear physicist, was a member, and our group asked him to talk with us, since we felt in many ways as he and the members of his group did.

At his very first meeting with us the guys prayed together and responded to God in a free manner. It was after this meeting that Zeke said, "If it takes m.s. to bring me to this, then I thank God I have it. Otherwise I might have continued to ignore God." It was here that I made a stronger commitment of myself to God.

Zeke and I continued to have talks. Once in a while we would go out for coffee and ice cream and talk for hours on end. His love for God and ice cream grew greater and greater. I used to kid him about eating so much ice cream.

Zeke liked to go to the beach whenever he could. When he went with some of the other fellows and they would play football or volleyball on the sand, he was usually unable to participate and would sit on the sidelines and talk to some of the bystanders. He didn't seem to mind this, however, as he was grateful just to be able to be there and take in the sunshine.

Zeke had to go back home before the opening of the winter quarter. He left without saying good-by. I understood and knew that was Zeke's way. Only occasional correspondence passed between us. Summer came and I was working as life-guard.

It was near the end of the summer that I got your call and found out he was gone. It hit me like a rock, but then I was "happy-sad." You know what I mean, I think. The rest of my feelings I think you are aware of. . . .

Zeke's testimony and life have meant a great deal to me and they will never be forgotten. I pray I will never take for granted what I have and I would live my life as if each day were my last.

The love between Zeke and Steve was much more than "glass threads or frostwork." On numerous occasions at school when Zeke was declining in health, he would rely on Steve to run errands or do other jobs which required physical strength. Steve's unselfishness on Zeke's behalf was demonstrated when the latter returned to Westmont without an assigned room and Steve gave up his own bed until proper accommodations could be found.

That the affection was mutual is borne out in a letter from Zeke I have in my possession, which urged me to mention Steve's name to the committee who makes choices of All-Americans in soccer. He said he was confident Steve would win a berth if his accomplishments as a soccer player were seriously reviewed.*

I have often thought about the other young men who shared in the meetings to which Steve referred. I have wondered whether God dealt with each of them as specifically as He did with Zeke and Steve and whether those dealings have borne fruit in their lives, and as a consequence, in the lives of still others. As we see, the life of one of them already taken from earth is reproducing its spiritual influence over and over.

* At the time of this writing Steve has made the U.S. Olympic team in soccer.

A
Dark Day
in August

7.

A Dark Day in August

THERE WAS NO SIGNIFICANT change in Zeke's condition in early August, 1969, although we noticed he had more difficulty in swallowing and he could not hear quite as well. His appetite continued to be normal and he could still walk forward by holding on to my arms. Reaction to the cortisone caused his mind to race and he could sleep for only short stretches at a time. We had already begun to use less of the cortisone, for we were convinced that the unfavorable side effects recently experienced outweighed any benefits it might contribute. Zeke's ankles were quite badly swollen, but the physician attributed this to continued inactivity.

Then on Saturday morning, August 9, he awoke and complained of headache. He said he would like to have coffee right away. I helped him into the chair by his bed and he ate a light breakfast. Getting some food and liquids into his system would usually cause his headache to abate, but this morning he continued to complain of pain in his head and he decided to lie down again rather than transfer to the liv-

101

ing room. He had lain down for only a few minutes when he became nauseated. When he showed no signs of relief, we called our physician.

Our regular physician was not on call, but his alternate agreed to come to the house early in the afternoon. When he examined Zeke, he showed no undue alarm. He said that upsets of this kind were not unusual, though he cautioned us to keep a wary eye on the fever.

Later that afternoon Zeke vomited several times quite violently. By evening he had calmed down, but registered some fever. We kept close by his side, giving him as many liquids as we could. By this time he was unable to talk loudly enough for us to make out what he was saying, but when we asked whether he wanted to drink or to roll over he would nod in reply.

By midnight his breathing was more laborious and his fever registered 102°F. We called for one of our friends who was a registered nurse to check him and to advise us what to do. His breathing was accelerated and he appeared only semi-conscious. "He's a very sick boy," she said. "I believe you should call his doctor again; I'm sure he would order him to the hospital." Since it was about one A.M., we decided to continue liquids and aspirin to combat the fever until early morning, as his temperature was still holding at 102°F. At six A.M. I called the doctor and within thirty minutes the ambulance had transferred him to Central DuPage Hospital, where he received oxygen and intravenous feedings immediately.

I was scheduled to speak that very Sunday morning at a church in nearby Lombard. Substitutes are quite difficult to get in August, when most of the Wheaton faculty are away on vacation, and it seemed quite unfair to call someone on the spur of the moment. Moreover, I have always disliked to disappoint a congregation, so I decided to go ahead and speak as scheduled. Before I left the hospital to go to the church, the doctor met me in the hall and gave me his pessimistic prognosis, "I'm afraid this is terminal."

It is impossible to explain how one keeps his bearings under such circumstances. When I began to falter as I contemplated standing before a congregation of morning worshipers, June spoke to me resolutely. "Zeke would want you to keep your appointment. He is in God's hands and God will give you strength to do your task." How I did it, I do not know. But I spoke to the audience that morning on faith in the inscrutable ways of God. Quite obviously I spoke to myself as much as to the people to whom I ministered. They did not know of my heartache that morning. I had shared the news of my son only with the leader of the church service, and I asked him not to make a public announcement of it to the congregation, as I was fearful it would be distracting. The strength that bore me up that morning was not my own.

Zeke's unconsciousness and elevated temperature continued in the afternoon. Ice packs and other medication afforded only temporary relief. By evening the fever held at 105°F. Members of the hospital staff did everything within their power to bring it down, virtually packing him in ice. Our regular physician, Dr. Paul Parker, who had learned that morning through an announcement made in church of Zeke's admission to the hospital, came directly to our side and gave his personal assistance in Zeke's battle for life. None of us thought the end would be as near as it was. "This could go on for several days," the doctor said.

A few of Zeke's intimate friends were admitted to his bedside during the afternoon. I stood quietly by Chuck Glasser, one of Zeke's closest friends, as he looked with pained countenance upon the unconscious face of his lifelong playmate and bosom companion. Chuck's heart was too full to speak.

I understood. How well I remembered their playing whiffle ball for hours on end in the park across the street, their trudging together to and from school, their laughter and chatter in our home, their common association in a multitude of interests. We had grown accustomed to seeing Zeke go out our front door and start north and knew he was heading for Chuck's. The Glasser family was large; but Zeke felt in that family a warmth and welcome he loved to share in. My arm went around Chuck as I spoke what I thought was appropriate for the moment. "He is ready for whatever God wants. That must be true of us, too."

Later in the evening some close friends of our family volunteered to watch by Zeke's side while June and I drove home briefly to get some needed things for the night. We had scarcely gotten inside our door when the phone rang and a voice said, "Zeke has taken a turn for the worse. The nurse thinks you should come at once."

I remember little of what immediately followed. Our short drive back to the hospital seemed interminable, although in reality it was only a few minutes. Three nurses were watching over Zeke as we entered the room, but in a glance I knew that our boy was treading the narrowest end of the isthmus which divides life from death. Gone was the oxygen tank, the intravenous feeder, the packs of ice, the feverish flurry of the nurses. Our boy was beyond human help and was edging away from us who loved him to the great Lover of Souls who was calling Zeke to Himself. I saw a beautiful, peaceful face, transformed by the radiance of eternity, tilt slightly upward on the pillow and breathe effortlessly two or three times. Then our boy was with the immortals. I saw him go; I did not call after him, although one of my choicest possessions had left this world. I knew he had clasped the angel's hand securely and now his spirit was taking flight to mingle with cherubim and seraphim and joining with the spirits of just men made perfect in a better world. He left behind his once strong, young body that had been decimated by disease and racked with pain but that would be transformed in the glad day when body and spirit would be reunited.

> Evening Star . . . the darkness beyond twilight,
> And then for him the white ship drew to shore.
> None saw the sails or heard the sound of oar,
> But while we watched, with heartstrings tensely drawn,
> Faith's valiant hero bravely ventured on the silent craft where stood the Mystic Rower.
> The homeward-turning tides took up and bore the ship away
> Like some full-breasted Swan,
> Along a lane of dazzling light
> To that fair port which knows not sin or death or pain or endless night.
> There, the voyage done, the radiant guest is robed in shining white,
> His day of endless rapture has begun. [20]

For an instant, I felt an impulse to follow. If I could only behold what he did in that moment! I knew what the hymn writer was trying to express when he said,

> If we could but climb where Moses stood
> And view the landscape o'er,
> Not Jordan's stream, nor death's cold flood
> Should fright us from the shore. [21]

Heaven was in that hospital room. The ineffable glory which engulfed us all banished grief and brought an indescribable joy. One nurse turned uneasily to June and requested her to step out into the hall, for a physician had to be summoned to make the final pronouncement of death, and it is not unusual for people to lose all composure at a deathbed, especially the immediate members of the family. When the nurse exhorted her the second time, June spoke clearly, without undue emotion, "Leave now? Why? We're Christians. We have lived for times like this. We're not afraid." Again, God's presence filled the room.

All who stood nearby were visibly moved during those moments, although there was a noticeable absence of weeping. A spirit of serenity, triumph, quiet beauty prevailed. No one present would question that God had a hand in what had just transpired.

Missed immeasurably during those final hours was the strong support of our son Jim. Not expecting an emergency to develop as quickly as it did, he and his wife Dotty were on a short trip overseas. Since we knew the detailed steps in their itinerary, we were able to reach them by telephone. June's brother got Jim on the line in Zurich, Switzerland. Jim was hardly prepared for the dramatic turn of events. "Be good to my parents," he enjoined his uncle. Immediately he and Dotty flew to our side.

Corky also was absent at the end. Concluding the last phase of a summer study-term abroad, she received in London the news of Zeke's serious illness. Although she took a plane immediately to Chicago, she did not arrive in time to see him alive.

"Precious in the sight of the Lord is the death of his saints," says the psalmist. [22] I had read about the peaceful death of the righteous. Records of Christians' deaths abound in notes of praise, victory and assurance. Often today we do not choose to look death squarely in the face as in other times, but are dulled by opiates or turn on our heel when the last minute on earth approaches. But "Blessed are those who die in the Lord." I agree with Robert Browning's exhortation on death in his poem "Prospice":

> I would hate that death bandaged my eyes, and forbore,
>   And bade me creep past.

No! Let me taste the whole of it, fare like my peers,
    The heroes of old,
Bear the brunt, in a minute pay glad life's arrears
    Of pain, darkness, and cold.
For sudden the worst turns the best to the brave,
    The black minute's at end,
And the elements' rage, the fiend voices that rave,
    Shall dwindle, shall blend,
Shall change, shall become first a peace, then a joy,
    Then a light. . . .

Christians do not fear death. It is graduation day. Especially when one feels that God has a direct hand in it, death is glorious. For reasons unknown to us God wanted Zeke now. We know that God is fashioning the Church, the body of Christ, to conform to His image. Each of us who knows Him has a unique place to fill. Zeke's work here must have been accomplished more readily than most people's and God needed him for something special in the ultimate Kingdom. Hence his days here were short. As one of my colleagues wrote to us, "God must have loved him very much to have poured into his young life so much of Himself and to ask him to suffer and then to call for him personally to attend to a work which He needed to have done now."

I await anxiously to discover the kind of mission Zeke is on, the special task he is performing. What a head start he is going to have on me! When I contemplate what has happened, I realize how closely this life is intertwined with the next. More decidedly than ever before I want my days left in this world to count for those things which transcend time.

And yet I weep on occasion — without shame. Intellectualize as I may, I still get caught in the throes of grief. Surely, this is a "vale of tears." The godly can suffer acute pain, sorrow, and longing. One of the consolations we received contained the words of Psalm 34:18, "The Lord is nigh unto them that are of a broken heart." I realize excessive mourning evidences self-pity, but I believe God sympathizes with us in our human condition and understands. Perhaps it is selfish to say that we will miss Zeke greatly, that there will be a vacant chair, that we shall not be able to share any more in his goals and achievements or his joys and sorrows or witness the fulfillment of his plans and life purpose. Maybe I am conceding too much to my humanity and engaging too much in selfish concern, but I would not be honest if I did not admit that occasional torrents of anguish threaten to overwhelm my soul. Spirits of deep depression press in uninvited and cling like tentacles to the spark of life. Of course, we know that Satan is the author of discouragement and despair and that he ranges only within the permissive will of God, but to deny the recurrence of poignant seasons of grief would be to deny reality.

At times I am unable to shake off the grim realization that Zeke was unable to achieve what are considered the normal expectations of life: education, marriage, involvement in world affairs, discharge of long stewardship to God. No doubt Satan has taken advantage of me as I have dwelt upon this unnatural aspect: he was too young to die. Why a promising young life of nearly twenty-two years? I know many other mothers and fathers have asked the same question about the inordinate loss of their sons on foreign battle fields or by accident or disease. Usually war takes some of our finest young men. If someone must die, why not the indecent, unambitious, God-rejecting reprobate who neglects his family and contributes no positive good to the world? Why not the murderer, the avenger or the whoremonger? Or, at least, why not one of those who has longed and prayed for death as a sweet release from bodily infirmities?

Wilma Burton, a very dear friend of Zeke's, wrote the following poem when she learned of his passing:

God's Love-way Is Best

He is too young to die! I cried.
And would have driven death aside,
This lad stands at the brink of life. . . .
Must he know death's serrated knife?
Heaven does not count her time
As we, but has a clearer chime. . . .
A truer clock with main-spring wound
By sun and star, by quiet pound
Of lunar tide and ocean swell.
When Heaven rings her homing knell,
The heart must stay its loud protest
And know that God's Love-way is best.

Does weeping arise from loving? I recall that Jesus wept at the grave of a very dear friend. The suggestion that He wept at Lazarus' grave because of the unbelief of those who stood around is not a satisfactory one for me. Once I accepted that exegesis, but when I think of our Lord identifying Himself with frail humanity, I believe He was touched by the grief of others who mourned. Jesus loved Lazarus. I don't understand it all, but Jesus was mysteriously and wonderfully human. Because this is a vale of tears, tears become an integral part of the human predicament. But I read of One who will one day wipe all tears from our eyes. [23] And "weeping may endure for a night, but joy cometh in the morning." [24]

Of course we must go beyond tears. As one of our friends wrote about the imminent death of his own sister, "To succumb to too much emotional concern on my part would suggest that I loved her more than Him." He took courage from God's words in Isaiah 43:4 (RSV), "You are precious in my eyes, and honored, and I love you. . . ."

Of the lessons God would teach us, none are more vivid than those learned through first-hand experience. If the grace of God must penetrate as deeply as ingrained sin, then the deliverance which God brings to pass must encompass as much territory in our lives as the disruption. How comforting for the person being tried in the furnace of sorrow to experience God's adequacy.

When Jesus said, "Be of good cheer, I have overcome the world," He indicated the source and the power of supernatural help. To pass from darkness to light or from night to day, from the terrestrial to the celestial or from the human to the Divine, from doubt to faith or from sorrow to joy — this is accomplished by the power of One who stilled the tempest and healed the leper and turned water into wine and rose from the grave. God works out His eternal purpose through both life and death.

"I Will Lift Up Mine Eyes Unto the Hills"

8.

"I Will Lift Up Mine Eyes Unto the Hills"

THE DAY AFTER ZEKE DIED, our doorbell rang. It was Dr. Paul Parker, the physician who had been ministering so faithfully to us over the many preceding weeks. Keenly aware of the shock death can produce upon immediate members of the family, and compassionate by nature, he had come to offer words of consolation and to check on the well-being of each one.

I remember vividly how this unusual man drew up a chair beside June and me and began to talk about spiritual matters. Here was a skilled physician, whose working days are ordinarily filled with consultations and surgery, eager to speak about subjects of a higher order.

"I believe heaven is a place," he said as he looked out of our living room window to the athletic field beyond. Then lifting his eyes to the jagged tops of the distant pines bordering the field, he continued, "I mean a definite place — as real as the moon — a place where astronauts might go, if God willed that they should."

His face became animated and a light shone in his eyes as he turned toward us and continued, "I also believe that heaven is a place of pleasure. God has given us the capacity to enjoy such a variety of things. If heaven is a place of glorious fulfillment, then it must be a place where there are 'pleasures for evermore.'" He paused a moment and then added, "I mean, of course, a place of worthy pleasures — those which will fully satisfy our spiritual natures."

The conversation that followed centered upon the solid realities of life in which he believed. My brother-in-law, a dentist from Pennsylvania who, with his wife, had come to our side when they heard of Zeke's death, was also present. He, too, was a vital Christian, and conversed with Dr. Parker about the opportunities for witness each had in the American Medical Society, as well as in the day-to-day routine of their respective professions. For about an hour our thoughts were lifted above death to the hills beyond.

As he stood to go, Dr. Parker turned to June and me with these words, "If Zeke could not get well, God was kind to take him now rather than plunge him in a prolonged period of helplessness. He is with the Lord and that is far better."

My mind turned back to the last trip Zeke and I had made to Santa Barbara, when he drove me to some of the scenic spots he loved. A couple high points on the mountainside overlooking the sea stand out in my mind as his favorite places to come and sit. I, too, was struck with their beauty and took several pictures of them. The hills seemed to be a source of strength to him. Today, the Lord of the everlasting hills was his impregnable tower of strength.

Again, I recalled his words to his brother written shortly afterward from one of these lookout points: "When I feel low, I go to this spot on the mountainside overlooking the ocean and sit and think. It seems to pick me up." Also, I recall his visit to the summer sports camp in Connecticut when he spoke of his love for the hills and natural surroundings. Even then he seemed to be seeking the vantage point of the high place. Today, he was scaling heights beyond mountain and ocean and sunset.

Hundreds of friends from far and near signed the registry at the funeral home. Flowers from churches, schools, relatives and friends poured in, although we requested in lieu of flowers that funds be directed toward a memorial gift to the English department of the College or to the Multiple Sclerosis Society.

Most of all we desired that the final hours before interment reflect a Christian outlook. Naturally, we appreciated the sympathy expressed by friends during the hours of visitation, as at other times. On the other hand, we did not want to give the impression that we viewed the grave as a terminus rather than a gateway to a better life. Periodically my eyes turned to the handsome face as it slept peacefully amid the floral tributes and I mused, "This very body will one day put on incorruption, as will mine. Everything points to the fields and hills beyond. . . ."

At the close of the first night of visitation I noticed a pink carnation nestling on Zeke's arm close to his side. I guessed at once who had put it there, for it had come from Corky's arrangement of flowers which were resting directly beneath his head. The flower would wither, but the love which it represented will survive the ravages of time.

It was fitting that the memorial service be held in the college chapel. Although it was August and many people were away on vacation, the East Chapel was well filled.

The dominant note was one of triumph. Zeke's pastor and close friend Allyn Sloat spoke briefly, with feeling, of his association with Zeke in the youth activities of the church and of the times he had counseled with him in spiritual

matters. Dr. Evan Welsh, the college chaplain, also a close
friend of Zeke's, read selections from Romans 8, Second Corinthians 5, and Revelation 21 and 22.

> For I reckon that the sufferings of this present time are
> not worthy to be compared with the glory which shall be
> revealed in us. . . . The creature itself also shall be deliv-
> ered from the bondage of corruption into the glorious liberty
> of the children of God. For we know that the whole crea-
> tion groaneth and travaileth in pain together until now. . . .
> We ourselves groan within ourselves, waiting for the adop-
> tion, to wit, the redemption of our body.

> For we know that if our earthly house of this tabernacle
> were dissolved, we have a building of God, an house not
> made with hands, eternal in the heavens. For in this (taber-
> nacle) we groan, earnestly desiring to be clothed upon with
> our house which is from heaven. . . . For we . . . groan . . .
> that mortality might be swallowed up of life. . . . We are
> confident . . . and willing . . . to be absent from the body,
> and to be present with the Lord.

> And I saw a new heaven. . . . and I John saw the holy
> city, new Jerusalem, coming down from God out of heaven,
> prepared as a bride adorned for her husband. And I heard
> a great voice out of heaven saying, Behold, the tabernacle
> of God is with men . . . and God himself shall be with
> them. . . . And God shall wipe away all tears from their
> eyes; and there shall be no more death, neither sorrow,
> nor crying. . . . And his name shall be in their foreheads.

The chaplain's comments stressed the importance of pre-
senting our lives fully to God as the source of heavenly peace
and power — even as our Lord has said, "My meat is to do
the will of him that sent me, and to finish his work." [25] The
words of an Archbishop of Canterbury, who also had known
grief from personal loss, were cited:

> Bereavement is the deepest initiation into the mysteries
> of human life — an initiation more searching and profound
> than even happy love. Love remembered and consecrated

by grief belongs more clearly than the happy intercourse of friends to the eternal world. It is proved stronger than death. Pure affection so remembered and so consecrated carries us beyond the bourne of time and place altogether. It transports us into a purer air where all that has been, is, and will be lives forever in its true being, meaning, and value before the throne of God.

"This experience of sorrow," said the chaplain, has been a profound initiation into the deeper meaning of life . . . for Zeke and . . . for his family . . . for the girl who visited him regularly but who knew in her heart that barring a miracle she and Zeke would never know happy married love. . . ."

Dr. Welsh quoted some excerpts from Zeke's own writings as the latter approached death: "Although I am only twenty-one and have experienced but a short period of the average life, I feel . . . the gigantic importance of finding the ultimate meaning to life. Death is as much a part of life as living. No one can escape it. Fear of it is only human, but I have found an assurance that truly overcomes fear. . . . Meaning for me has come unhypocritically . . . through a personal relationship with the God-man, Jesus Christ. . . ."

"Someone has said we should count time by heart-throbs rather than by figures on a dial," the chaplain continued. "God took Borden of Yale at twenty-four, Robert M'Cheyne at twenty-nine, Frederick Robertson at thirty-six. Our Lord died at thirty-three. At twenty-one Zeke has left his testimony and blessed our hearts because his life was given to Christ. . . ."

Then the chaplain read the tribute which I wrote shortly after Zeke died:

The Angel of Mercy bent low last Lord's day evening to reclaim the spirit of our younger son whose years with us in this world seemed altogether too brief. There was no demurring to the summons, no faltering, no fear. The once strong, young body, racked with pain and ravaged by a baffling and overpowering physical enemy, called death sweet names as restoration and healing did not seem to be in God's plan.

The weeks of Erwin's (Zeke's) confinement enabled June and me to know him even better than before, for he inclined more and more to share his thoughts and insights as we cared for him daily. Disability did not drive a wedge between him and God but rather moved him to reassess and adjust his values and to place high priority on spiritual concerns. Again and again he spoke of the transitoriness of life and the temporality of money and earthly possessions and the enduring quality of love for man and love for God. He grew to appreciate even more the beauties and pleasures we often take for granted: the glory of the sunset above Old Lawson Field, the tint of the roses which grew outside his back door, the frolic of the dog in his neighbor's yard. He loved the mountains and the sea and made them his close companions during his school days in Santa Barbara. His life was brightened only a few days before his death by a trip to the hills of Pennsylvania, where he will return for his final resting place on earth.

His zest for and knowledge of sports have always been among his best-known characteristics.

He grew to be an avid reader. As he withdrew from physical activity he turned his attention to reading as his strength allowed — always with reflection and critical evaluation. The intensity of his days called for application of belief and understanding of truth to practice, and personal commitment. His appreciation for God's Word grew, and it was always a joy to converse with him about the implication of the passages which he read. Constantly we were struck with the maturity of his insights and originality and thoughtfulness of his interpretations. His determination and indomitability are attested to by his completing seven hours of college credit during the current summer session.

He said only a few weeks ago that if he recovered his health, although he sensed no specific call to the ministry, he nevertheless felt compelled to do personal witnessing directly to his friends more than in the past. He disliked hypocrisy in any form and determined never to profess above his possession. His prayers were never long but were marked by candor and sincerity. By nature socially inclined, he made friends readily; nevertheless he cultivated and cherished the close friendship of a select number who knew him most intimately. His utter honesty has often challenged June and me to scrutinize more closely our motives for action, for he was quick to detect selfish motives clothed in altruistic garb.

As many pure spirits of the past have been refined by suffering, so the enigma of Zeke's suffering could only be resolved by acceptance of the divine purpose. Naturally he loved life and remained hopeful of recovery to the end. However, his hope was tempered by occasional comment on death's imminence and the fulfillment of God's will by his affliction. His sensitive manner and gratitude for every act done on his behalf made a joy of every daily ministration. Also his wry, but irrepressible sense of humor never deserted him unto the end.

As it is impossible today to take full measure of the sweet memories which Zeke leaves, so it is impossible to give adequate thanks to the host of students and to the faculties of Wheaton and Westmont Colleges, to the many friends. in Wheaton where he has grown up, to the various churches and individuals over the country who have reassured us constantly of their prayers and abiding concern. June and I both have felt the constant undergirding of a strength beyond our own. The God who made his homegoing triumphant has never failed to sustain. Things of earth grow a little more dim today and the purlieu of heaven is much brighter as this precious jewel is returned to the Divine Jeweler for safekeeping. "Great and marvellous are thy works, Lord God Almighty; just and true are thy ways, thou King of Saints." We say with another of old, "The Lord gave and the Lord hath taken away. Blessed be the name of the Lord." Good-by for now, dear, dear son. But please be on the lookout . . . we will meet you in the morning.

Few tears were in evidence at the service, for God seemed very near. Full realization that Zeke was ready to meet God banished even momentary sorrow and left joy in its

wake. Prospect of a new and better day to come shone forth
brightly. That Christ's resurrection was the prophecy and
potentiality of our resurrection broke in anew upon our consciousness.

Zeke's cousin, Andy, sang "Face to Face" and followed
with a favorite of Zeke's, "Mine Eyes Have Seen the Glory."
The confident and hopeful words of that song lifted the
hearts of every one. One who attended said afterward, "God
was truly there; I've never seen a more victorious service."
A Catholic friend was heard to comment, "No one could attend that service and not be a better person as a result."

Seven of Zeke's close friends, acting as pallbearers, carried
him lovingly to the hearse which transported him to O'Hare
Airport for the last leg of his earthly journey. That evening,
a jet plane swept him away into the azure blue toward the
hills of northern Pennsylvania for his final resting place on
earth. Because it was terrestrial, the body could not follow
the spirit which had taken a nobler flight, but even then his
celestial voice was blending with others from afar, whose
sound was "as the sound of many waters."

A local mortician met his body at the Buffalo air terminal
and accompanied it to Bradford. A few personal friends and
local relatives, including Zeke's grandfather, joined the last
family gathering at Oak Hill Cemetery and trudged up the
steep incline to the burial spot. There a local pastor-friend
read from the Scriptures and committed his body to the
earth.

High up and overlooking this picturesque Pennsylvania
city, the grave faces hopefully and expectantly the direction
of the rising sun, where one day the Sun of Righteousness
will rise with healing in His wings. How fitting for Zeke's
body to be placed again on the vantage point of the high
place to await the resurrection. "I will lift up mine eyes unto

the hills, from whence cometh my help. My help cometh from the Lord, which made heaven and earth." [26]

At the very time the graveside service was being conducted, Dean Peter Veltman was delivering a convocation address to the graduates of the summer school in Edman Chapel. Challenging them to align their lives and purposes with worthy standards, he said, "Man, being the creature he is, ultimately faces two alternatives — death and life. The type of protest I encourage will enable him to face either. I would like to conclude with the record of a protest of a Wheaton student who has faced both. Last Sunday I stood at the bedside of Zeke . . . in Central DuPage Hospital, as his bodily forces fought valiantly to supply him with life-sustaining air. A member of the class of '69, aged 21, promising in physique and mind, Zeke had taken seven hours of college work this past summer amid physical odds that would have deterred all but those who have a profound commitment to One greater than themselves. Just prior to departing this life Zeke wrote, 'When it comes to emotional feelings and a personal relationship with God, each individual is as much an expert as the most highly educated intellectual. With this in mind, I feel as highly qualified as anyone else to express my ideas on a normal Christian life, since I have experienced personally the emotional thrill and assurance of a vital relationship to God, through Jesus Christ. I can expertly attest to the benefits of the Christian life . . . for it is the only life with meaning. . . . ' Today Zeke is being buried in Pennsylvania."

His
Continuing
Witness

9.

His Continuing Witness

OF ONE THING I am sure: our son's early death was not meant to diminish the impact or silence the influence his life was to have upon others. One of the inexorable laws of nature dictates that life comes out of death. "Except a corn of wheat fall into the ground and die, it abideth alone: but if it die, it bringeth forth much fruit." [27] Even as life eternal came out of the death of our Lord, so the lives of many may be helped in an unusual way through the divinely-appointed death of one person.

I have been struck again and again by the impact his death has already made upon other young people. When the President of Wheaton College read excerpts from Zeke's writings to the student body, many responded by notes, letters, and personal comments.

A local athletic coach who attended the funeral spoke to some athletes later about the example of this athlete who was ready to die. He asked whether they, too, were "running the race" for God and ready to die. Although they were physically strong today, none of them could be sure of a long life, he said. Two of the boys were touched by the appeal and indicated a full commitment of their lives to God.

A young man wrote to us concerning his unbelieving brother, "I am convinced that not only will I see Zeke in heaven, but from what my brother has said of Zeke's death, I will see him there too."

Since Zeke's passing, I have had occasion to talk with many students in my office, in the halls, and in the classroom about what death means and how it relates to them. Sometimes for class devotions I speak of our personal encounter with death and how our young son had to face it. Students seem to appreciate my willingness to share my experience with them. A few of them have told me of their own sorrows. One young man told me of the death of his older brother from an incurable disease. A girl shared with me the loss of a brother in an accident. Our burdens provide a mutual basis for understanding and compassion.

The college newspaper carried excerpts of Zeke's writings at the beginning of spiritual emphasis week, with the editor's note, "May Zeke's words be a challenge and inspiration to all of us as we enter these days of spiritual renewal."

Of those who have written to tell how their lives have been affected by his death, only a select number can be included. Here is an excerpt from a letter written by a close college friend . . .

> . . . I must admit that the most astounding element about Zeke's illness was the resultant change in his attitude toward purpose in life. My early contact with Zeke left me with the impression that he had a relationship with God, but none which stimulated him into expressing it with any-one. . . . I visited him frequently upon his return to Whea-

ton and observed his physical deterioration, but I was also strengthened in my faith, as I never heard him complain.

The conviction that dominated the last days of his life was that so many of us in the Christian sub-culture resign ourselves to a nominal Christian experience, never getting to the place where we really desire the more-abundant life.

I can never fully understand the why of the death process, but I really feel that God worked mightily through Zeke's ordeal, and although death was the end of it, I believe God was the ultimate victor because of the "good" derived from his inspirational struggle.

Levi Edgecombe

Later, when Levi graduated and joined the staff of a church on the West Coast, he wrote:

I deeply appreciate the two papers you gave me which Zeke wrote just prior to his passing. The high schoolers went for a week-end ski camp in January, and in preparation I read to them Zeke's paper on "A Normal Christian Life." Because I had known Zeke and was able to relate the tremendous change in his concern for spiritual values, the kids were very sobered. Thanks again for the papers, because they were so helpful in demonstrating the importance of using our time here on earth, especially when the end of our existence is unknown.

From a very dear, lifelong friend, who knew Zeke as well as anyone:

When we all lost Zeke, I lost a true friend. For me to say this is to describe fully how I knew him and the special relationship that existed between us. There is an honesty and openness between friends which can result only from trust and confidence. Each depends on and implies the other. To "know" an individual is to see him as he really is, not as he would have others to believe he is.

To know Zeke was to know a person who could see through the dishonesty, inconsistency, or insincerity of others. Regarding spiritual matters, he was unable to believe anything a person said when it was not borne out in the life of that person. I knew Zeke as one who was unable to reconcile the Christianity he heard preached with that which he saw around him. Our doubts concerning Christianity were grave indeed as we grew up together.

But it was this same intolerance of inconsistency and pettiness that enabled Zeke shortly before his death to discover his God in reality. Zeke learned what most people never do — that the way to God is difficult, not easy. To have known this person is to have known a most extraordinary one — as a friend with whom I grew up, and as one who found God in spite of those who stood in his way.

Chuck Glasser

From another of Zeke's cherished friends of long standing:

It is now almost a year since I last spoke to Zeke. I have often reflected on what he meant to me and on the rare qualities that made him a valued friend. I knew him as classmate, teammate, and close friend for nearly ten years, from the carefree days we spent as boys on the ballfield to the last weeks of his life when we could only talk and share the pleasure of each other's company on those rare occasions when his strength would allow. There are a thousand memories. To fully express what they mean to me now is impossible.

I remember him mostly as a trusted, reliable friend, something difficult to analyze or put into words, yet personal and deeply felt. I recall his genuine, unpretentious honesty, a rare quality which I appreciate even more now as I remember him. Even while fighting a hopeless battle against an incurable illness, he wanted to experience life as best he could, and to enjoy the company and conversation of friends. Devoid of pretense of any kind, he never tried to impress others or impose his values on them. His faith and values were rarely articulated or expressed, but revealed in subtle ways to those who knew him well. His sense of values didn't really change near the end. He just saw things a little more clearly than before.

Only those closest to him could fully appreciate the faith

and acceptance he showed in those last few years. At no time was Zeke morbid or self-pitying. He wanted only to make the most of what he had, for as long as possible. I was often amazed by his patience with those who didn't know or understand. When someone made an unthinking remark about the patch he wore over his eye, he was understanding — far more understanding than I could have been, preferring to save them the embarrassment by not explaining or discussing his illness. He had no desire for pity or special treatment, keeping the gravity of his condition a secret from all but a few. I remember his determination in those final years to be active and alive and happy, even when his illness had robbed him of his strength — how in the final months when even talking had become difficult, he strained to enjoy a short visit from a friend.

When Zeke discussed his religious faith, he showed a simple, yet deeply sincere belief. I remember a day at the lake a couple summers ago when we sat in a boat and talked about things so often ignored or passed over. Our conversation touched on the meaning of life and the world around us. He said, "I just believe there has to be something more than this. Life has to have some meaning beyond what we have here now." Knowing him as I did, that is how I would have expected him to say it, a simple expression of how he felt and what he believed. I recall most vividly those days at the lake — relaxed, quiet times when we could talk and think and enjoy the outdoors. Zeke was very ill by then and his strength almost gone, yet he laughed and talked and for a while seemed to forget. Occasionally his mood would change and he would be serious and reflective, and at times even hopeful. Though he knew there was no cure, he retained a firm hope that his illness could be slowed down or arrested. He talked of marriage, of teaching, of settling in Florida, of what could be done despite his increasing handicap, of the pleasure he could find in simple things that had taken on new importance.

And yet he was prepared to face the worst. He confided that he could accept it as God's will, that it wasn't really the end. I often wondered had I been in his position whether I would have had his faith, or his courage to live with such a burden and accept my fate, to enjoy life and even laugh as he did. I think often of his laughter, how even near the end we could talk and laugh together, how he could put aside his problems and enjoy himself. I can only think it was because he was at peace with himself.

Don Hoppe

An excerpt from one of Steve Gay's letters states: "I think of Zeke a lot when I drive around in Santa Barbara. Places remind me of him. Also, when I think of God, I am reminded that Zeke died living a life that was 100 percent for God. This at times helps me over the little problems that I find. It is still very much a bumpy road as far as spiritual things are concerned, but it is, and has been, worth it."

Tom Dykstra, Little All-American in basketball at Wheaton College, wrote, "When I came to Wheaton, Zeke and I spent a lot of time together, as our interests were very similar. . . . When I first heard of his death, I was taken aback. How tragic! I thought. Why Zeke and not me? I asked myself many times, and still do today. . . . The only answer I can give is that God wanted him for Himself. Zeke faced up to his commitments to Christ in a way no man without God's peace could have done. His passage into a new life is a triumphant reward."

Corky wrote:

Dear Dr. and Mrs. Rudolph:

I would love to have a part in the memoir to Zeke, but where do I start? How can I put down the thoughts that have run through my mind since he died? How can I put into words the impact this relationship has had on my life?

Zeke and I knew each other for a year and a half. This is a comparatively short time, but in looking back, it seems that I have known him most of my life. We became so close before he died that it is hard to remember what things were like before I met him and much more difficult to imagine what they would have been like if I had not.

In many ways Zeke was an amazing boy — or should I say an amazing man, for in several ways he was both a boy and a man. When we first met, I thought he was a crazy, mixed-up boy, but before he passed away I could honestly say that here was a man of God.

Sometimes he was downright stubborn, or as he would probably put it, "just sure of my convictions." This was a good quality, for it made him analyze all aspects of a problem before making up his mind. This carried over into his spiritual life; all his doubts were very serious, and it took him awhile to willingly let God rule in his life. But once Zeke made up his mind, there was no doubting it. Now he was God's man, no matter what the consequences.

It was amazing to watch his deepening commitment in the face of increasing physical disability. The same stubbornness, or determination not to give up, was evident in the way he fought against his disease. Often I wondered whether I would have been able to keep my spirits up as he did if I were in his place. But I know now that God gives strength just when we need it and not before. God gave him strength day by day just as He has given me strength since. I am sure, Dr. and Mrs. Rudolph, that you have found this to be true in your own suffering.

Even though Zeke was overcome by terrible weakness, he drew upon God's resources for his emotional and spiritual stamina.

Being very close to him, I learned in a new way to trust God day by day rather than to look far into the future. He and I could not be sure of a future together, so we *had* to go a day at a time, enjoying each other in the day at hand. God gave each of us joy, for Zeke and I learned to look to God for His way, His will, His strength.

In many ways it seems that all of this happened ten years ago. My perspectives have changed greatly. I was such an earthbound Christian before. For Zeke to be taken away so soon has made me realize more than ever that I am only a sojourner here; my true home is with my Heavenly Father.

I realize anew that the only important things here are being right with God and accomplishing things for Him.

Zeke has gone. Only God knows how long any of us may have to live. But we know that in God's time all of us will be together.

With love always,
Corky

Zeke's voice comes not only through the words of concerned friends, but also through statements which Zeke made directly. The following selections are from two papers written for a college class in Christian Doctrine, July, 1969. He died August 10th.

A NORMAL CHRISTIAN LIFE

. . . In a culture where Christ's teachings have become commonplace, many lose sight of the real message being expressed. A Christian, or Christ-one, should be separated from the world, as Christ taught, and not merely a moral part of it. . . .

It is with a great deal of zeal that I attack what I have coined "infant Christians." Growth through Christ by practice, prayer, and communion with Him is vital to the normal Christian life. One must not stagnate on the line of conversion if he intends to give meaning to his new form of life. . . . Once man has received the saving knowledge and emotional experience of God's grace, his desire for true growth in Christ beyond a conversional status should overwhelm him to seek out the same for others. Some people seem to be "converted" almost every week. This Christian immaturity can be a hindrance to others as they examine the normal Christian life for its possible acceptance. Overemotional infant Christians, who each week-end share their "mountaintop" experiences and then drag during the week, often leave would-be listeners very cold. Herein lies the importance of true growth and progress in the Christian life for the benefit of witness to the unsaved. . . .

Legalism is not the answer. . . . The fullness and happiness of communion with God through the man Jesus Christ seems to become lost in a maze of moral rules to be strictly followed. The following of these moral teachings is important, but only secondary, and will come naturally through the seeking of the will of God after one has received the saving power of God's grace. . . .

. . . When it comes to emotional feelings and a personal relationship with God, each individual is as much an expert as the most highly-educated intellectual. With this in mind, I feel as highly qualified as anyone else to express my ideas on a normal Christian life. Since I have experienced personally the emotional thrill and assuring feeling of a vital relationship with God through Christ Jesus, I can expertly attest to the benefits of the Christian life. If properly applied through God's transcending love beaming through us, the Christian life can and should be the happiest and most assuring life, for it is the only life with meaning. Each person must strive through prayer, personal devotions, and through God's text, the Bible, to better himself. Fellowship with other Christians, as well as yearning for the saving of others, will necessarily follow. This combination of faith and the love of God shining forth in our lives is the essence of what I feel should be the normal Christian life.

WHAT IS MEANINGFULNESS?

. . . Some men seem to have more time than others to ponder the meaning of life and the realities of existence. Some are more sensitive by nature or because of hereditary or environmental factors. Others less sensitive by nature are caught more in the modern humdrum mode of the everyday suburbanite. . . . The music of a child's laughter, the fragrance of a rose, the charm of the sea, the majesty of the mountains ignite in the sensitive spirit dark, disturbing wonderings about the meaning of it all. . . .

Modern man's values, as I view them, are typically of a secular nature. The "God is dead" concept of the twentieth century seems to be a means to ease the conscience and deaden the senses of the soul of the average man. Churchgoing is more popular than ever but seems to hold less meaning and purpose than formerly. Social ties and pleasures within the church appear to have risen above messages of the supernatural and separated life. We can note evi-

dence of this further in the synthetic rise of the new moral-
ity. (This misplacement of values has been aptly described
as really just the "old immorality.")

This deadening, pleasure-seeking trend of life and blotting
out of ultimate concerns has not been without serious consequences for modern man. His built-in fear of death and
what follows, if anything, still haunts him. Analysts' couches,
suicidal attempts, tavern attendance, and the use of drugs
have been cowardly attempts to drown out this innate haunt-
ing of the soul by what is really meaningful. Life has to
be more than materialism, but where do we find modern
man looking for something beyond it? Bigger cars, bigger
houses, pensions, financial securities, luxuries, and constant
spending on counterfeit ideals mark just a few of man's pursuits of meaning. This may be an overly-dark general picture of modern man's secular, hardened soul; however, this
is how I picture the direction which our society has taken.

This materialistic and blasé way of squandering through
life is undergoing a vast inventory and criticism most evident in our youth movements. The spoon-fed youth, though
spoiled by a materialistically successful, but soul-deadened
society, seems to be searching for ultimate values and trying
to find meaning somewhere. Though seemingly misdirected
and confused ninety percent of the time, movements such
as radical college students, hippies, flower-children, and the
increasing numbers of runaways indicate the discontent of
our youth.

Further illustration is in the way our youth are influenced
by modern musicians. For example, the Beatles, who for a
time sought the mystical religions of India and drew many
young people after them, later had a devastating effect on
the faith of the youth when they rejected God and the
supernatural. John Lennon's statement, 'I'm as popular as
Jesus Christ,' depicts this movement away from faith. Such
albums as 'Magical Mystery Tour' and 'Sergeant Pepper's
Lonely Hearts Club Band' and the later Beatles' reference
to the man who believed in God as 'the fool on the hill' depict this rejection.

It is most regrettable that in their search for meaning the
youth have been misled by the bad examples when there

was such potential for the right. Before it is too late and they have thrown their lives away, the youth of today want to know the "score" instead of wasting precious time and health on what they consider to be the worthless goals of their predecessors. Our youth seem to be taken up with a more ultimate view of meaning, though their answers often prove to be immature. Their visions, however, are commendable. . . .

. . . Although I am only twenty-one and have experienced only a portion of the average lifespan, I feel a definite sensitivity to the gigantic importance of finding the ultimate meaning to life. Death is as much a part of life as living. No one can escape it. Fear of it is only human, but I have found an assurance that truly overcomes this fear. It is a true belief in a supernatural God. This was not a blind leap, nor was it logical reasoning totally, but an overcoming feeling brought on by something much greater than myself. . . . Meaning cannot be found inwardly in a humanistic manner, but it seems to me that it has to be poured in outwardly. Each individual has to open himself up and unlock his soul, using more than his mind to find meaning. Meaning for me has come unhypocritically and honestly through a personal relationship with the God-man, Jesus Christ. To me, He is Being itself. I do not consider this mere emotion, but a reality. Christ's teachings have brought meaning to my life, not in a legalistic or moral way, but through an inspired feeling and assurance of their validity.

A verse that God's inspired text, the Bible, has brought meaning to me is Romans 12:1. . . . This verse has real relevance as to the communion with the Supernatural. . . . My life on earth should exemplify to others and to myself Christ-likeness. The separation and meaning that I have received through this communion cannot be a selfish direct pipeline to God, but must involve an attempt for others to experience meaningfulness, too.

Another verse that has significance for me regarding life here on earth and the relationships of which I have been speaking, is Romans 1:16, "For I am not ashamed of the gospel of Christ, for it is the power of God unto salvation to everyone that believeth; to the Jew first, and also to the

Greek." Here is meaning to me. It is only through God and the outward and inward pouring of His Spirit that there is meaning to life. This indescribable experience, in my opinion, can and should be experienced by anyone who has longing for ultimate values in his soul.

Understandably, the effect of Zeke's death on Jim has been very pronounced. Beyond the sadness of personal loss and shock from the unusually swift descent of the disease, he has undergone an acute, persistent anguish. As he said to me, "I think back to some of the brotherly 'spats' we had and how petty they seem now . . . I keep asking myself, 'Why him and not me?' I do not know the answer, but part of the reason must be that he was constitutionally better equipped to face such an ordeal than I. He was always the venturesome sort who was willing to tread the unknown, while I was one who had to have everything figured out and be in perfect control at all times. I doubt that I would have been able to bear what he did."

In another conversation with me, Jim reflected further on what Zeke's death had meant: "In all my efforts to achieve the doctoral degree, I realize now that self was the chief focal point. In the field of education one emphasizes social concerns, but I had not yet attached proper value to friendship or family ties. When death came, how quickly my priorities shifted. I remember how much Zeke relished people. He has taught me to belittle mundane and trivial pursuits and to set greater values on life's intangibles."

To Pastures New!

10.

To Pastures New!

And now the sun had stretched out all the hills,
And now was dropped into the western bay;
At last he rose and twitched his mantle blue:
Tomorrow to fresh woods and pastures new.

— John Milton, *Lycidas*

ONE YEAR HAS NOW PASSED since Zeke's death. Still, today, thoughts of that traumatic experience are never far from the surface of our minds. Time heals very slowly; the wounds are still gaping and the recollections are as sharp as the razor's edge. Our outward composure may belie the inner struggle, but even our zest for life returns only intermittently as something vital seems to have left us.

Recently a newscast featured an interview with several veterans of the Vietnam War, some of whom had lost limbs or eyes or were mangled in some other grotesque manner. The conversations revealed the heroic determination of these men to live actively in the future, but life could never be the same for them as they had suffered irreplaceable loss. Similarly, when you are joined by love to another and separation comes, something of you goes too. This is what John Donne speaks of when he says, "Any man's death diminishes me, because I am involved in mankind."

I find myself still grappling with the enigma of human suffering, especially in one so young. My mind continues to fluctuate between discomfiture and peace.

However, I have derived much strength from a careful look at the Scriptures themselves. As I observe God's dealings with His people to determine the reasons for suffering and death, I note that some pain is brought on by man's stupidity and wrong-doing, for which he can blame only himself. Again, I also discover that God may personally allow suffering to come upon us for reasons which please Him. When He does, we ought not to demur, for God knows what is best for us. "Let them that suffer according to the will of God commit the keeping of their souls to him in well-doing, as unto a faithful Creator." [28] We are even told to rejoice.[29] The chastening by God seems to remind us of our true sonship: "Whom the Lord loveth he chasteneth." [30]

God has even intimated why He chooses to chasten us. He says, for example, that Israel went through the trials of the wilderness to see what was in their hearts. Israel also needed to be weaned from the present world. Their enslavement in Egypt and the afflictions which followed made them ready to depart when the time came. After the Babylonian captivity, many of the people of God chose the comforts of their new environment to the inconvenience of returning to their land; hence they had to be dealt severe measures.

Whatever God is doing in and through those who love Him, He makes it clear that He is fashioning His vessels into the image of His Son. [31] The affliction may be severe, still it is "but for a moment" and secures for us an "eternal weight of glory." [32] And those who have suffered most are able thereby to comfort others. [33]

Even though a person may note some of the reasons for adversity, he still does not win the spiritual battle automatically. In the first place, he is not always sure what precept applies to him, for he lacks God's perspective. When the course of natural events is reversed violently, he is driven to say, "Lord, I do not understand, but surely You do, and I trust You because I love You. As I am Your child, surely You control what happens to me. I must not lose sight of You, for I will need reassurance in my weakness." And "Shall not the Judge of all the earth do right?" [34]

During the past year I have come to know a little more of what God is like. Although I can never comprehend His character fully, I agree with Adam Clarke's eloquent comment that He is ". . . a Being who, from His infinite wisdom cannot err or be deceived, and who, from His infinite goodness, can do nothing but what is eternally just, right, and kind." [35] Here we are reminded that God is good. Whatever He lets happen is for the best. We must believe that whatever happens to His children is meant for their good. "All things work together for good to them that love God. . . . " [36]

One of the most debatable lines of Alexander Pope, found at the close of Part I of his *Essay on Man* reads: "Whatever is is right." Readers do not usually swallow this wholesale unless it is fitted into the context of a deeply committed Christian life, for only there can one say whatever happens to him is necessarily for his good and for God's glory. When one is not God's child, his willfulness may take him far from God's preferences. However, if one is given to God and serving Him diligently, whatever happens to him will result in good, if not immediately, at least ultimately, for God is good. For the "goodness of God leadeth . . . to repentance." [37]

I have learned anew to accept unequivocally the sovereignty of God. Nothing really gets out from under His control. He is accomplishing His purposes in the world. He has a plan for each of us. At times, mysteriously, He intervenes in human affairs and switches things around to realize His ultimate goal. Although I believe firmly in man's free moral agency and God's response to prayer, sometimes God, for reasons not yet known to us, points directly toward someone and says, "I have chosen you for this hour" — whether it is to become king or a leader to perform a specific task or even perchance to die, as it suits the Divine Purpose.

One fact emerges clearly: God had a hand in what happened to our son. He answered prayer.

On numerous occasions I have listened to stories of dramatic healing in response to prayer. I have listened with rapt attention and gratitude to others tell of God undertaking for them in times of crisis. I, too, can testify of times when it has pleased God to arrest affliction. But God's response to prayer for Zeke, though he was spared the direst extremes of his disease, lay in producing in him a more sterling Christian character rather than in sparing his life. Death was not to be averted, and we must accept that verdict as God's way. God delivers *in* adversity always; He may or may not deliver *from* it. "In the world ye shall have tribulation: but be of good cheer; I have overcome the world." [38] When the Apostle Paul prayed for a physical impediment to depart, God told him, "My grace is sufficient for thee . . . my strength is made perfect in weakness." [39] The genius of the Gospel is not that we shall escape trouble, but that we shall have strength to endure it.

The principle of selectivity in prayer defies human comprehension. Sometimes those who are in strategic places of service, who are supported by prayer, are cut down mysteriously. Peter was delivered miraculously from prison when prayer was made for him; yet he died a martyr's death about thirty years later. When adversaries persecuted James, he was not spared a martyr's death; however, the records abound with illustrations of God's miraculous interventions for others. One is driven inevitably to say, "God has done this thing. We will not question Him." Even as the author of First Kings stated, "Thus saith the Lord, Because the Syrians have said, The Lord is God of the hills, but he is not God of the valleys, therefore will I deliver all this multitude into thine hand, and ye shall know that I am the Lord." [40]

June and I have consoled each other many times. When we have read of a young person who despairs of life because of drug addiction or another bringing disgrace on himself and his family through immorality or murder, we realize that some things are worse than death. When we read of one like Lord Byron who burnt out his life in sinful indulgence and wrote in his diary at thirty-five that he regretted to have lived so long and to so little purpose or of the unbelieving Voltaire whose dying words at eighty-four were, "I am about to take my last voyage — a great leap into the dark," we realize that death itself is comparatively irrelevant and length of life is of secondary importance. "Let me die the death of the righteous."

One of the most permanent impressions made upon me is that something has happened of cosmic and eternal significance. What happened to our son is bound up with the future, the coming order, the permanence of life. The resurrection now takes on new significance. I find myself looking forward to the great climax of the Lord's return and the consummation of all things.

I do not agree with those who maintain that a life lived here in accord with Christian precepts would be worthwhile apart from a future life. Life in this world is inextricably bound up with the next and really makes no sense without it. The tone of our existence here is conditioned by our expectations that personality will continue beyond the grave. Joys of earth yield satisfaction only as they attach themselves to permanence and immortality. Again Paul comments, "If in this life only we have hope in Christ, we are of all men most miserable." Celestial voices hymn it into our souls and accompanying harps, by angel fingers touched, sound forth the song of our great immortality. No truth known to man is more meaningful or thrilling than that of the Resurrection. He is risen! I, too, shall rise! I will be united with Him and with my son and with the great company of believers who have gone on ahead! What a day that is going to be!

Intimations of what lies ahead tease one's imagination. "Eye hath not seen, nor ear heard, neither have entered into the heart of man, the things which God hath prepared for them that love him." [41] Even now, we may take comfort in the extravagant promise of Paul that " . . . neither death, nor life . . . nor things present, nor things to come . . . shall be able to separate us from the love of God. . . . " [42]

Today it is new pastures for Zeke. In a way I, too, must turn my back on the past and look to the "green fields" and "pastures new" of the future, for that is where he is. God has a work for Zeke to do in the new kingdom; He also has a work for me to do here until He returns to earth.

Many times I have theorized about the future. I have wondered just where Zeke's departed soul might be — at what "rill" might he be stopping or what "oaten flute" might he be playing or what "quill" would he be trying. I have even wondered whether the souls of departed saints might be engaged in carrying out Divine missions, as God says of the angels, "are they not all ministering spirits, sent forth . . . ?" [43] Thus, they would go in and out among us, though unseen. But my thoughts of these things are conjectural, for what can I fathom of heavenly existence?

". . . neither hath entered into the heart of man, the things which God hath prepared for them that love him." [44] Our knowledge, therefore, is fragmentary. If God had thought it necessary for us to know more about these matters, He would have told us more.

I wrote earlier of heaven as being a place. I also believe it to be a place of dynamic development — not of static existence. The ditty that says about the afterlife, "Don't mourn for me now, don't mourn for me ever / I'm going to do nothing for ever and ever" speaks a mistruth. A beautiful medieval dream-vision called *The Pearl* tells of a poet who had lost his pearl (a child) in the grass on a bright August day, but when he fell asleep and dreamed, he saw his child on celestial soil just across a narrow stream. As he talked with her, she explained that heaven does not consist of mere pastoral joys or sequestered ease. Rather, it is founded on dynamic growth and development in the service of God. The poet noticed that his child had grown since he had last seen her. Such a vision coincides with my view of death and the afterlife. One thousand years from today I shall have advanced in every way. But I do set the direction of that development in this life.

I shall not call the circumstances which cut our son down so early a tragedy. To do so would be to malign the God who has shaped events in his own way. Our calculations were altered, but God's plan was unfolding. Our son has turned to green pastures of new achievement. Death signaled merely a transfer to a new sphere of action. Who can belittle the service he is now performing? Who will claim that the unusual turn of events here marks the unnatural circumstance rather than the natural?

One point emerges clearly now: God had His hand on all of Zeke's life — from the early days when God gave him to us, through our dedication of him to God, through his own conversion — to his death. Although some periods of Zeke's life were more marked by spiritual fervor than others, I can never remember him as irreverent or unreceptive to the Gospel. However, little that we did as parents deserves merit. God's mercy and love, which dealt faithfully with him all his life, came one day to reclaim the gift which had been loaned to us temporarily.

Thomas Gray said in his famous *Elegy Written in a Country Churchyard* that those who died young and lay buried in the graveyard were spared the many sorrows which were common to man. I find only vague comfort in these words, unless I know that God has directed the decease of each one there. While this world is a "vale of tears" ravaged by sin, to assert flatly that one is better off dead is to question the wisdom of God in delaying His second coming and sparing man's life further in a world of protracted woe. One must believe with Browning, "This world is no blot nor blank. It means intensely and it means good."[46] God must see that the total good which accrues from continuation of the world under His plan outweighs the apparent relief which would ensue from ending all life now, or we could challenge God's administration of all things. However, if God wills that a life cease now, then that is good — not so much because it is spared disease or war, but simply because God's wisdom has directed it.

Again and again one is driven helplessly into the arms of God as he seeks surcease from sorrow. One of my editor friends wrote me recently, "The older I grow, the less confident I am that I have explanations for why God does what He does. . . . Moses knew the ways of God because he knew the works of God. So there are intuitions about the way God works that can come to a Christian in the course of time which he can trust. But I suppose that on this side of the eternal dimension the 'why' will always be partially blank."

Recently I stood on the Mount of Olives overlooking Jerusalem. As I looked beyond the Mount of Ascension and the Garden of Gethsemane and across the Kidron Valley, toward the city, I was thrilled to think that Christ will personally set foot again in that region. As I beheld the Golden Gate, which is now sealed but which the inhabitants say will be opened at Christ's Second Coming, I said in my heart, "Even so, come quickly." Many things there and elsewhere will be set right when He returns. Ideologies of men will cease jarring against each other. Men will no longer be scattered as sheep without a shepherd. God will in that day transform our lost battles into final victory.

But faith searches for a resting place now.

Many times I have read and partially proved, "My grace is sufficient for thee. . . . My strength is made perfect in weakness. . . . My peace I leave with you." But during the special days of trial in the death of our son, I have proved with my heart the truth of God which before I had acquiesced to only mentally.

The effect of Zeke's death has resulted already in a refinement of my own soul, an acceleration of my spiritual energy, a sharpening of my perspective. It would be most unfortunate if I had let such an ordeal pass without discerning God's supernatural power at work. I have prayed many times with David, "Open thou mine eyes, that I may behold wondrous things out of thy law." [46] Many times Zeke has said, "I wonder whether God is letting this happen to me to teach somebody a lesson." Many of us have learned more intimately the secret of walking close to God.

Today I live more than ever with eternity in view. I see "fresh woods" and "pastures new" even in the faces of young people whom I teach. Continuity of life — even the life of my son — goes on in them and extends to the future. Young people in a special way embody strength, vision and hope. They overcome all obstacles and press toward goals yet unattained. But when I speak to them of one of their number who died young, believing that the quality of one's life is much more important than its length, they listen attentively to the lesson it holds for them.

Meanwhile, I must do the unfinished work assigned me and conform to God's image. That will require patience. "Those who bear His mild yoke . . . serve him best. . . ." [47] But we labor and wait knowing that our Father loves and cares, for He more than any other realizes what it is like to give up a Son.

To the Christian there is always tomorrow. Hope for a happy reunion in a better world lights up the future. This hope is based on Christ's resurrection. And every man "that hath this hope in him purifieth himself. . . . [48]

Now our expectations are in the "fresh woods" and "pastures new" of immortality. Zeke has gone ahead to those green fields of glad service, while we remain to work here a little longer. But the lure of those fields from afar helps to wean us from thoughts of earth.

Now we see more clearly:

> Death begins with birth;
> Life begins with death —
> Glorious fulfillment!

FOOTNOTES

Preface

[1] II Timothy 1:10
[2] Isaiah 55:9
[3] I Corinthians 13:12

CHAPTER 2

[4] Matthew 4:3

CHAPTER 3

[5] I Corinthians 10:13
[6] Isaiah 43:2 (RSV)
[7] Colossians 1:17
[8] II Corinthians 12:9
[9] Proverbs 31:10

CHAPTER 5

[10] II Corinthians 4:9
[11] Matthew 11:12
[12] James 5:16
[13] Matthew 17:20
[14] Psalm 73:17
[15] Acts 12
[16] Acts 2
[17] Matthew 18:20
[18] John 11:40
[19] "Departed Friends" by Henry Vaughan

CHAPTER 7

[20] Poem by Samuel Porter. The first line only has been emended to fit the time of day Zeke died.
[21] Isaac Watts, "There Is a Land of Pure Delight"
[22] Psalm 116:15
[23] Revelation 7:17
[24] Psalm 30:5

CHAPTER 8

[25] John 4:34
[26] Psalm 121:1, 2

CHAPTER 9
27 John 12:24

CHAPTER 10
28 I Peter 4:19
29 I Peter 4:12, 13
30 Hebrews 12:6
31 Romans 8:29
32 II Corinthians 4:17
33 II Corinthians 1:4
34 Genesis 18:25
35 Commentary, vol. 1, p. 27
36 Romans 8:28
37 Romans 2:4
38 John 16:33
39 II Corinthians 12:9
40 I Kings 20:28
41 I Corinthians 2:9
42 Romans 8:38, 39
43 Hebrews 1:14
44 I Corinthians 2:9
45 "Fra Lippo Lippi"
46 Psalm 119:18
47 John Milton, Sonnet "On His Blindness"
48 I John 3:3